The Trial
of Sacco
and Vanzetti

FAMOUS
TRIALS

Other books in the Famous Trials series:

The Trial
of Sacco
and Vanzetti

by James Barter

FAMOUS
TRIALS

LUCENT BOOKS

An imprint of Thomson Gale, a part of The Thomson Corporation

THOMSON
™
GALE

Detroit • New York • San Francisco • San Diego • New Haven, Conn.
Waterville, Maine • London • Munich

© 2005 Thomson Gale, a part of The Thomson Corporation.

Thomson and Star Logo are trademarks and Gale and Lucent Books are registered trademarks used herein under license.

For more information, contact
Lucent Books
27500 Drake Rd.
Farmington Hills, MI 48331-3535
Or you can visit our Internet site at http://www.gale.com

LIBRARY OF CONGRESS CATALOGING-IN-PUBLICATION DATA

Barter, James, 1946–
  The trial of Sacco and Vanzetti / by James Barter.
    p. cm. — (Famous trials)
  Includes bibliographical references and index.
Contents: The crime and the investigation—The prosecution: the case for old Yankee America—The defense: blaming Red Scare hysteria—The fight to escape the electric chair—The case that will not die.
  ISBN 1-59018-549-8 (hard cover : alk. paper)
  1. Sacco, Nicola, 1891–1927—Trials, litigation, etc. 2. Vanzetti, Bartolomeo, 1888–1927—Trials, litigation, etc. 3. Trials (Murder)—Massachusetts. I. Title. II. Series.
  KF224.S2B37 2005
  345.73'02523'09744—dc22
                                   2004022142

Printed in the United States of America

Table of Contents

Foreword

"The law is not an end in and of itself, nor does it provide ends. It is preeminently a means to serve what we think is right."

William J. Brennan Jr.

THE CONCEPT OF justice and the rule of law are hallmarks of Western civilization, manifested perhaps most visibly in widely famous and dramatic court trials. These trials include such important and memorable personages as the ancient Greek philosopher Socrates, who was accused and convicted of corrupting the minds of his society's youth in 399 B.C.; the French maiden and military leader Joan of Arc, accused and convicted of heresy against the church in 1431; to former football star O.J. Simpson, acquitted of double murder in 1995. These and other well-known and controversial trials constitute the most public, and therefore most familiar, demonstrations of a Western legal tradition that dates back through the ages. Although no one is certain when the first law code appeared or when the first formal court trials were held, Babylonian ruler Hammurabi introduced the first known law code in about 1760 B.C. It remains unclear how this code was administered, and no records of specific trials have survived. What is clear, however, is that humans have always sought to govern behavior and define actions in terms of law.

Almost all societies have made laws and prosecuted people for going against those laws, but the question of which behaviors to sanction and which to censure has always been controversial and remains in flux. Some, such as Roman orator and legislator Cicero, argue that laws are simply applications of universal standards. Cicero believed that humanity would agree on what constituted illegal behavior and that human laws were a mere extension of natural laws. "True law is right reason in agreement with nature," he wrote, world-wide in scope, unchanging, everlasting. . . . We may not oppose or alter that law, we cannot abolish it, we cannot be freed from its obligations by any legislature. . . . This [natural] law does not differ for Rome and for Athens, for the present and for the future. . . . It is and will be valid for all nations and all times.

Cicero's rather optimistic view has been contradicted throughout history, however. For every law made to preserve harmony and set universal standards of behavior, another has been born of fear, prejudice, greed, desire for power, and a host of other motives. History is replete with individuals defying and fighting to change such laws—and even to topple governments that dictate such laws. Abolitionists fought against slavery, civil rights leaders fought for equal rights, millions throughout the world have fought for independence—these constitute a minimum of reasons for which people have sought to overturn laws that they believed to be wrong or unjust. In opposition to Cicero, then, many others, such as eighteenth-century English poet and philosopher William Godwin, believe humans must be constantly vigilant against bad laws. As Godwin said in 1793:

Laws we sometimes call the wisdom of our ancestors. But this is a strange imposition. It was as frequently the dictate of their passion, of timidity, jealousy, a monopolizing spirit, and a lust of power that knew no bounds. Are we not obliged perpetually to renew and remodel this misnamed wisdom of our ancestors? To correct it by a detection of their ignorance, and a censure of their intolerance?

Lucent Books' *Famous Trials* series showcases trials that exemplify both society's praiseworthy condemnation of universally unacceptable behavior, and its misguided persecution of individuals based on fear and ignorance, as well as trials that leave open the question of whether justice has been done. Each volume begins by setting the scene and providing a historical context to show how society's mores influence the trial process and the verdict.

Each book goes on to present a detailed and lively account of the trial, including liberal use of primary source material such as direct testimony, lawyers' summations, and contemporary and modern commentary. In addition, sidebars throughout the text create a broader context by presenting illuminating details about important points of law, information on key personalities, and important distinctions related to civil, federal, and criminal procedures. Thus, all of the primary and secondary source material included in both the text and the sidebars demonstrates to readers the sources and methods historians use to derive information and conclusions about such events.

Lastly, each *Famous Trials* volume includes one or more of the following comprehensive tools that motivate readers to pursue further reading and research. A timeline allows readers to see the scope of the trial at a glance, annotated bibliographies provide both sources for further research and a thorough list of works consulted, a glossary helps students with unfamiliar words and concepts, and a comprehensive index permits quick scanning of the book as a whole.

The insight of Oliver Wendell Holmes Jr., distinguished Supreme Court justice, exemplifies the theme of the *Famous Trials* series. Taken from *The Common Law*, published in 1881, Holmes remarked: "The life of the law has not been logic, it has been experience." That "experience" consists mainly in how laws are applied in society and challenged in the courts, a process resulting in differing outcomes from one generation to the next. Thus, the *Famous Trials* series encourages readers to examine trials within a broader historical and social context.

Introduction

Politics on Trial

O N APRIL 15, 1920, two innocent men were murdered in a small Boston suburb during a bungled armed robbery. Crimes of this sort were not uncommon at a time when the nation was struggling to recover from the hardships of World War I. Many men returning from the war were still unemployed; many more toiled long hours at low-paying factory jobs to feed and clothe their families. Petty crime was common, and violent crime was on the rise. Little about the murders was reported in local papers until three weeks later, when police announced the arrests of two poor Italian immigrants, one a shoemaker and the other a fish peddler.

Shoemakers and fish peddlers do not often make the headlines, but these two did. Within in a few days, Nicola Sacco and Bartolomeo Vanzetti were identified as known anarchists who publicly advocated the overthrow of the government and took part in violent labor strikes in Boston. By the time of their trial, one year later, both had become household names in the United States. By the time of their execution seven years later, their case had gained international notoriety and their names were permanently linked in history.

The Red Scare

Sacco and Vanzetti's fame stemmed not from their crime but from their radical politics, which collided with the more conservative politics of most Americans, and from their immigrant status. The prevailing attitude, in light of the agonies and sacrifices of the war and the potential threat of Communist and anarchist conspiracies, was one of intense patriotism and xenophobia, or fear and mistrust of foreigners. Public intolerance and official disregard for civil rights were fueled by high levels of immigration and news of political upheaval elsewhere in the world. In this climate economic uncertainty, combined with a wave of bombings, violent strikes, and spectacular anti-American rallies, triggered the public panic known as the Red Scare.

The clash of mainstream American conservatism and anti-American extremism had its roots in the end of Word War I and the Communist Russian Revolution of 1917. At that time, American troops were just returning from Europe. Germany had been defeated, and most Americans savored the sense that the country was now safe from the imperialism of Kaiser Wilhelm and the communism of Lenin. Victorious troops returned to ticker-tape parades and flowers tossed by appreciative sidewalk spectators, and Americans looked forward to a return to prewar harmony and prosperity.

This optimism, however, was short lived, replaced by early 1919 with uncertainty, confusion, and irrational fears. The sudden and unforeseen terror that gripped Americans was the realization that America might be safe from foreign attacks but not from attacks from within. Several antidemocratic or anticapitalist political groups—principally Communists, anarchists, and Socialists—gained substantial followings and threatened to undermine political stability when the public had not yet recovered its sense of security.

These three groups were collectively labeled "Reds" because of the dominant red color of the Communist Party's flag. Although each group embraced a somewhat different political and economic philosophy, all openly advocated the overthrow of the U.S. government and justified the use of violence to achieve that goal. All also advocated the seizure and redistribution of private property, as had taken place in Russia. Private ownership of land and businesses was a basic concept of American capitalism, and such radical talk outraged many patriotic Americans who proudly dubbed themselves "Old Yankee Americans" to distance themselves from the Reds.

American troops who fought in World War I are welcomed home with a parade in New York. After the war, Americans hoped to return to prewar prosperity and security.

A Wave of Violence

The initial response of state and federal government to political dissent was watchfulness and caution. But in a matter of months, the ranks of dissidents swelled to alarming levels. Hundreds of thousands of immigrant workers who had recently lost their jobs to returning soldiers, for example, resented their sudden poverty and their families' desperate circumstances. Many other disaffected workers, citizens as well as noncitizens, also found an outlet for their complaints in these revolutionary groups. Many small labor unions representing low-paid factory, mine, and dock workers joined the Industrial Workers of the World (IWW), a powerful labor union more commonly known as the Wobblies. Headed by Bill Haywood and Eugene V. Debs, both of whom openly embraced the revolutionary ideology of the Socialist Party, the IWW organized nationwide labor strikes, many of which turned violent and led to hundreds of deaths. Although the strikes were aimed at securing better-paying jobs for the strikers, they crippled an American economy struggling to retool to peacetime industry.

Simmering tensions between the radical groups and the government increasingly boiled over into militant confrontation. In February 1919, some sixty thousand workers participated in a violent general strike in Seattle, Washington, that closed down

Members of the IWW in New York demonstrate in support of striking union workers in Colorado. Such labor strikes crippled the U.S. economy after World War I.

the city for five days. More strikes followed. The Boston police force went on strike, which led to looting and vandalism and resentment by the unprotected public. Federal troops sent in to quell the strikers opened fire with machine guns, and several strikers were killed. On September 13, Boston police commissioner Edwin Curtis fired the entire Boston police force and hired replacements who were themselves bitterly resented by ousted officers. On September 22, 365,000 steelworkers walked off their jobs, shutting down three-quarters of Pittsburgh's steel mills. Strikers were blamed for inciting riots that led to many deaths when mounted police fired into crowds armed with rocks and glass bottles. The strikes, coordinated by the IWW, were labeled by the Old Yankee Americans and conservative newspapers as crimes against society, conspiracies against the government, and plots to establish anarchism and communism.

Violent strikes escalated to bombings. On April 28, several package bombs were delivered to prominent persons around the country who had made decisions regarding immigrant workers that the Reds disliked. One bomb addressed to Senator Thomas Hardwick of Georgia blew off the arms of Hardwick's housekeeper and burned his wife's face. News of this incident led a New York postal clerk to notify authorities that sixteen similar packages had been set aside for lack of proper postage—all were found to contain explosives. In the next few days, eighteen more mail bombs were intercepted, twelve of which were addressed to high officials: Supreme Court Justice Oliver Wendell Holmes, the mayor of New York City, three senators, two congressmen, two governors, U.S. attorney general A. Mitchell Palmer, and multimillionaire industrialists J.P. Morgan and John D. Rockefeller. A second bomb intended for Palmer exploded in front of his Washington, D.C., home, damaging the front of the building, shattering windows, and killing the perpetrators. In all cases anarchist groups claimed responsibility. On June 3 the headlines of the *New York Times* read, "Midnight Bombs for Officials; Bombers Die at Attorney General's House; Two Victims at Judge Nott's House Here; Bombs in Boston, Cleveland, Pittsburgh." [1]

In 1919 Attorney General A. Mitchell Palmer was the target of mail bombs sent by anarchist groups. Palmer responded to the attacks with raids against Red organizations.

Suppressing the Reds

Palmer, as the top U.S. law enforcement official, had finally had enough. He ordered several federal raids, dubbed "Palmer raids" by the newspapers, against known Red organizations. Sidestepping the courts and ignoring standard legal procedures, Palmer led the first raid on November 7, 1919. Its primary focus was the

Federation of Unions of Russian Workers, 450 of whose members were arrested in twelve cities and immediately deported.

An even more aggressive raid followed on January 2, 1920. Federal marshals in thirty-three cities simultaneously raided offices of the Communist Party of America, the Anarchist Party, and the Communist Labor Party. More than four thousand suspects were arrested, and by May a total of ten thousand had been rounded up. The majority of these people were European immigrants who were not yet citizens and were summarily deported back to Europe, several hundred on the SS *Buford* alone, on a one-way trip to Russia.

The Red Scare began to take on an aspect of mass hysteria. Legislatures reflected the frenzy by passing ordinances against broadly and vaguely defined "Red Activities." Thirty-two states, for example, made it illegal to display the red flag of communism, and the New York legislature expelled five duly elected Socialist

Boston police officers pose with books seized from a Communist organization in a 1919 raid. Possession of revolutionary literature was illegal during the Red Scare.

assemblymen from its ranks. Anarchist newspapers in several cities were shut down without proper court authority, and anyone caught possessing or distributing anarchist literature was subject to arrest. The hysteria of the Red Scare was captured in one Tacoma, Washington, newspaper, which editorialized: "We must smash every un-American and anti-American organization in the land. We must put to death the leaders of this gigantic conspiracy of murder, pillage, and revolution. We must imprison for life all its aiders and abettors of native birth. We must deport all immigrants." [2]

Almost as quickly as the Red Scare appeared, however, it faded away. Beginning in 1921, many citizens and law enforce-

Immigrants arrested in Boston during a 1920 roundup of alleged Communists are shackled as they wait to be questioned by authorities.

ment agencies recognized that innocent people had been unjustly imprisoned, businesses had been illegally closed, and families had been split by the deportation of one parent. Unfortunately this realization came too late to influence the prosecution of the Italian immigrants and self-confessed anarchists Sacco and Vanzetti. In the aftermath of the trial and executions, it became evident that the trial had been sensationalized, polarizing Americans into those who believed Sacco and Vanzetti were justly executed because they had committed murder and those who believed they were unjustly executed because of their anarchist convictions.

It seemed everyone who read the papers or listened to the radio at the time debated the guilt or innocence of Sacco and Vanzetti. Few were indifferent. However, the debate ultimately swirled not around whether the two defendants were murderers but around fundamental unresolved social and political issues: Is a society obligated to tolerate immigrants who advocate the overthrow of their newly adopted government? Should immigrants enjoy the same rights as full citizens? When is violence justified for political ends? And, how can prejudice be minimized in the courtroom to render a fair and impartial verdict? These were the questions ferociously debated by the media, leading politicians, the faculties of elite universities, common factory workers, and families at their dinner tables.

Not only did the execution of Sacco and Vanzetti not resolve these larger issues, it did not settle the controversy over their guilt or innocence. Since the 1920s the debate over the guilt or innocence of Sacco and Vanzetti has continued. Legal scholars and crime buffs alike continue to review, reevaluate, and reassess the events that occurred that April afternoon in 1920 and the legal proceedings that followed, seizing on purportedly new evidence that favors one side or the other.

The trial of Sacco and Vanzetti continues to grip the imagination and stimulate debate. Although the case reflected American politics during the early twentieth century, the issues it raised remain in the forefront of American politics and justice in the present day.

Chapter 1

The Crime and the Investigation

E ACH THURSDAY MORNING the 9:18 train from Boston to South Braintree, a suburb of Boston, carried an iron strongbox containing a $30,000 payroll for the Slater and Morrill Shoe Company. Like clockwork, the strongbox was picked up by the local American Express Company agent, Shelley Neal. His job was to load the box onto his horse-drawn wagon and drive the team to his office on Railroad Avenue. There Neal turned over the contents to the Slater and Morrill paymaster, Frederick Parmenter, whose office occupied the same building.

On the morning of April 15, 1920, on the way to the office, Neal noticed a parked car that he did not recognize—a dark blue touring car, maybe a Buick. Thinking little of it, Neal walked to his office, opened the strongbox, and pulled out two canvas bags of cash, one for the shoe company's management building and one for the factory where the shoes were manufactured. Neal took the factory payroll bag, climbed an internal staircase, and dropped it off at the Slater and Morrill office, where Parmenter counted out $15,776, divided it among five hundred employee pay envelopes, and loaded the envelopes in two smaller iron boxes.

About three o'clock that afternoon, Parmenter and his guard, Alessandro Berardelli, walked out of the office and headed uphill on Pearl Street toward the production factory. The two men casually chatted as they carried the weekly payroll on their two-hundred-yard walk, the same walk they had made on hundreds of Thursdays. Parmenter carried a .32 caliber Colt and Berardelli a .38 caliber

Harrington and Winchester, just to be on the safe side, although neither man had ever had cause to draw his weapon. Each man had in his hands one of the iron payroll boxes.

The two had no reason to suspect that this payroll delivery would be any different from all the others. Within easy view of the factory, their pace slowed as they approached a set of railroad tracks, and they paused until a guard lifted the crossing gate. As they walked on, two men leaning against a rail suddenly stepped forward, drew pistols, and fired. Neither Parmenter nor Berardelli had time to react. Parmenter staggered to a gutter and fell, dying from a bullet to the chest. Berardelli crumpled to his knees with four bullet wounds. Seizing the two iron boxes, the shooters jumped into the back of a waiting car containing at least two other occupants. As the getaway car sped off, more shots were fired in the direction of the two victims.

When the police drove up to take charge of the crime scene, eyewitnesses gave brief descriptions of the two men. All agreed that the killers had spoken Italian and that the getaway car was a

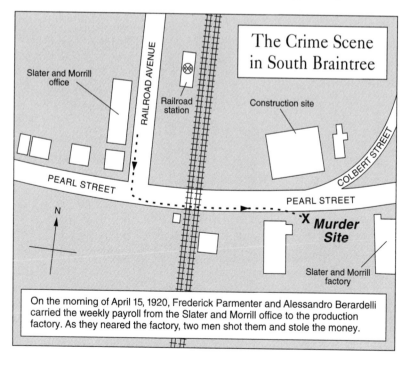

The Crime Scene in South Braintree

Slater and Morrill office

RAILROAD AVENUE

Railroad station

Construction site

COLBERT STREET

PEARL STREET

PEARL STREET

N

X *Murder Site*

Slater and Morrill factory

On the morning of April 15, 1920, Frederick Parmenter and Alessandro Berardelli carried the weekly payroll from the Slater and Morrill office to the production factory. As they neared the factory, two men shot them and stole the money.

dark blue touring car. James F. "Jimmy" Bostock, the first on the scene, handed the police four spent shells and a dark cap he found lying near Berardelli. From markings on the four shell casings, police identified the murder weapon as a .32 caliber Colt pistol.

The next morning the *Boston Herald* newspaper ran a banner headline that mistakenly reported the wounding of Parmenter and an incorrect dollar figure, "Motor Bandits Murder Guard, Wound Paymaster, Dash Away with $18,000." [3]

The Investigation

Two days after the crime, in a remote wooded area a few miles from South Braintree in the city of Bridgewater, two hunters came upon a dark blue Buick. They noted its missing license plates and a smashed rear window. Its appearance aroused their suspicions, and they notified police of their discovery. When police arrived to investigate, they discovered beside the Buick, which they determined had been stolen, the smaller tire tracks of a second car. The police suspected that the Buick might be the car involved in the South Braintree murders and that the tracks in the dirt might be those of a transfer car used by the robbers that could not be traced to the crime by witnesses.

The chief of police in Bridgewater, Michael Stewart, thought this discovery might be connected to more than one crime. Four months earlier, on December 24, 1919, a group of men driving what was described as a large dark blue touring car attempted but failed to pull off a similar armed robbery. Their target was a shoe company payroll, this time in Bridgewater, as the money was being transported. Witnesses to that crime scene described a shot-gun blast and robbers who spoke Italian. In age and general appearance their descriptions were similar, although not identical, to those of the murderers in South Braintree. Although no one had yet been arrested for the failed Bridgewater robbery and Stewart had no evidence directly connecting the two incidents, he could not ignore the similarities.

Stewart's suspicions sharpened when he looked into other local activity at the time of the Slater and Morrill murders. It so happened that April 15 was the date of the scheduled deportation of an Italian anarchist living in Bridgewater named Ferruccio Coacci—a man

NICOLA SACCO

Nicola Sacco arrived in Boston in 1908 at the age of seventeen. Clean shaven with a distinctive sharp jawline, he was nicely dressed as he disembarked from the boat in New York, a stylish characteristic that he cultivated all his life. He had been born Ferdinando Sacco in 1891, one of seventeen children in a fairly prosperous peasant family in a small inland town in southern Italy near the Adriatic coast. At fourteen he quit school to work in the fields, but his father had a friend living in Milford, Massachusetts, who was willing to take in the young man who hoped for a better life in America.

After arriving in Milford, Sacco's first job was as a water boy and steamroller oiler for road gangs paving asphalt that paid $1.15 a day. After a year or so, he took a better-paying job at an iron foundry and, in addition to working twelve-hour days, he attended English classes three evenings a week. Intent on accomplishing more than working in an iron foundry, in 1912

Nicola Sacco became involved with anarchism while working at a shoe factory.

Sacco applied for a job at the Milford Shoe Company. His skillful hands soon had him earning between thirty and forty dollars a week as a skilled shoe trimmer.

While working at the shoe factory, Sacco began attending anarchist lectures and social events. At a dance he met Rosina Zambelli, a quiet and pretty sixteen-year-old Italian girl, and the two were married. Within a year Rosina gave birth to their son, Dante.

well known to Stewart because of his militant politics. In preparation for his deportation, Coacci had quit his job at the Slater and Morrill Shoe Company. Coacci, however, failed to show up for his deportation on April 15. He called the Immigration Service the next day, saying that his wife was sick and that he needed a few extra days to take care of her. Immigration and police investigators found Coacci's story suspicious. First, Coacci's wife was not ill, and second,

Coacci was now insisting that he leave the country immediately. When police advised Coacci to leave some money behind for his wife and children, Coacci replied that they did not need any. On April 18, Coacci surrendered to immigration agents and boarded a ship departing for Italy the same day.

The day that Coacci's ship sailed, Stewart was digesting reports concerning the Buick discovered in the Bridgewater woods. He began to wonder if Coacci's dubious story about his wife's ill health, his recent employment at Slater and Morrill, and his sudden eagerness to return to Italy indicated some kind of involvement in the South Braintree holdup and murders.

The Getaway Car

Stewart decided to follow up on his hunch and made a second trip to Coacci's rented home. A man named Mario Buda answered Stewart's knock and allowed Stewart to look through the house and a rear shed. Buda explained that he kept his car, an Overland, in the shed but that it was currently being repaired at the Elm Street Garage. Stewart slid the shed door open, looked in, and observed something only a seasoned investigator would have noticed. The tire imprints in the dirt floor of the shed appeared too large for an Overland, but might be about right for a larger Buick.

On May 1, increasingly certain that there was a connection between the murders and Coacci, Stewart returned to look for Buda, only to find the house vacant, its occupants and furnishings gone. With a growing sense of urgency, Stewart decided to stop by the Elm Street Garage on the remote possibility that Buda's Overland might be there. It was. Excited by his discovery, Stewart told the garage owner, Simon Johnson, that if anyone tried to pick up the Overland, he should try to stall the owner and call the police immediately.

On May 5, a little after nine o'clock in the evening, Buda and three other Italians came to the Elm Street Garage to pick up the Overland. Following Stewart's instructions, Johnson sent his wife, Ruth, to call the police. Buda, who seemed uneasy, suddenly turned and walked with one of his companions to a parked motorcycle, and the two sped away. The other two men departed in the direction of a nearby streetcar stop and boarded the 9:40 streetcar from Bridgewater to Boston.

The Arrests

The men were gone when Stewart and his officers arrived, but on learning that two men had departed on foot to the streetcar, the policemen headed for the streetcar's next stop, Brockton. At 10:04 the streetcar pulled into the Brockton station. Two officers boarded the car and removed two men who seemed to fit the description of the men who had walked away from the Elm Street Garage. The men, speaking broken English with heavy Italian accents, gave their names as Nicola Sacco and Bartolomeo Vanzetti. A police

Bartolomeo Vanzetti (center, front) and Nicola Sacco (far right) are handcuffed to Boston police offers as they are escorted to the courthouse.

BARTOLOMEO VANZETTI

Bartolomeo Vanzetti was born in northern Italy in 1888, where he grew up in poverty. He established a reputation as a boy with quick fists, yet he was quiet at home and enjoyed reading. Although he might have achieved success as a teacher or lawyer, his father apprenticed him in a pastry shop, where he worked until 1903 when his mother died and he departed for the United States.

A committed anarchist, Bartolomeo Vanzetti urged workers to strike for their rights.

Through connections with other Italians, Vanzetti found work in Boston washing dishes and hauling garbage twelve hours a day just to make ends meet. Following one year of such drudgery, he wandered aimlessly around New England digging ditches, laying bricks, and leveling dirt roads, all the time sleeping in barns and on rooftops.

In 1914 Vanzetti moved to Plymouth, Massachusetts, where he lived with a family of anarchists while working in a rope factory. It was there that he committed himself to the anarchist movement and began speaking and using his literary and oratory talents to publish pamphlets and speak out urging workers to strike. In May 1917 Vanzetti fled to Mexico at the urging of anarchist leader Luigi Galleani to avoid being drafted into the U.S. Army. It was there that he met Nicola Sacco.

When the war ended, Vanzetti returned to America but continued his wanderings. First he went to St. Louis, then Ohio, and finally back to Plymouth, where he bought a pushcart and began peddling fish. Even on good days he never made enough money for decent housing, food, or clothing, and he never married.

search of the men revealed each was carrying a loaded pistol. Sacco's weapon was a .32 Colt. Vanzetti also carried in his pocket a printed flyer advertising a nearby anarchist rally that read:

> Proletarians [workers], you have fought all the wars. You
> have worked for all the owners. You have wandered over all

the countries. Have you harvested fruits of your labors, the price of your victories? Does the past comfort you? Does the future smile on you? Does a future promise you anything? Have you found a piece of land where you can live like a human being and die like a human being? On these questions, on this argument, and on this theme, the struggle for existence, Bartolomeo Vanzetti will speak. Admission free. [4]

By 10:15, Stewart had made up his mind that Sacco and Vanzetti were tied to the Elm Street Garage, Buda, Coacci, the dark blue Buick, and the murders of Parmenter and Berardelli. Stewart placed both men under arrest for carrying concealed weapons and took them to the Bridgewater police station for further questioning. He also issued a warrant for the arrest of Buda.

Interrogation

Stewart hoped Sacco and Vanzetti would incriminate themselves as at least accessories to the murders during interrogation. Once in the police station, Stewart arranged for District Attorney Frederick Katzmann, a man more skilled at interrogating suspects, to conduct the questioning.

When asked to explain his possession of a loaded .32 Colt, Sacco said that he had intended to harmlessly discharge the loaded gun but other responsibilities had prevented him from doing so. By this time, ballistics experts had already told Katzmann that the bullets that killed Berardelli had been fired by a .32 Colt. Although Katzmann could not know whether it was Sacco's .32 Colt, he found the coincidence significant. Vanzetti, who told his interrogators that he was an independent fish peddler, explained that he carried his pistol for personal protection from robbers who plagued small businessmen with pockets full of cash. When asked where he got the gun, Vanzetti said he had bought it at a store but could not recall which store, or when, or how much he had paid for it.

Both Stewart and Katzmann continued the interrogation. Both suspects denied being at the Elm Street Garage or knowing Buda or Coacci. When asked to account for their whereabouts on

April 15, the day of the murders, Vanzetti said he could not remember what he did that day and Sacco said he had been at work at the Circle-K Shoe Factory, where he had been employed for two years.

In Katzmann's opinion, the men were not credible. The anarchist flyer found on Vanzetti, and suspected association with other Italian anarchists such as Buda and Coacci, prompted Stewart to question Sacco and Vanzetti about their political beliefs, even though such beliefs had no direct bearing on the robbery and murder. At the height of the Red Scare, any ties to anti-American activity were cause for suspicion.

"Are You Anarchists?"

Katzmann, more than Stewart, counted himself a patriotic Old Yankee American, and he had openly expressed contempt for anyone, particularly recent immigrants, who condoned anarchy, especially the overthrow of the U.S. government. Concerned that this robbery might have been a conspiracy to raise money for a known local anarchist group, Stewart questioned both suspects about possible ties to the anarchist movement and their attitudes toward the U.S. government:

> Stewart: Are you a citizen?
>
> Sacco: No.
>
> Vanzetti: No.
>
> Stewart: Are you an anarchist?
>
> Sacco: No.
>
> Vanzetti: Well, I don't know what you call him [it], I am a little different.
>
> Stewart: Are you a communist?
>
> Sacco: No.
>
> Vanzetti: No.
>
> Stewart: Do you like this [the U.S.] government?
>
> Sacco: Yes, some things I like different.
>
> Vanzetti: Well, I like things a little different.

Stewart: Do you believe in changing the government by force?

Sacco: No.

Vanzetti: No.

Stewart: Do you subscribe to literature or papers of the Anarchist Party?

Sacco: Sometimes I read them.

Vanzetti: A man gave some to me in Boston.[5]

Katzmann had heard and seen enough. As the clock neared midnight on May 5, based on all evidence gathered, he placed both men under arrest for the murders of Parmenter and Berardelli.

Pretrial Hysteria

News of the arrests spread quickly, and public opinion was soon divided. The major newspapers represented the conservative views of Old Yankee America. Many rushed to publish banner headlines of the arrests accompanied by detailed if not accurate descriptions of Sacco and Vanzetti's radical backgrounds as anarchists. A May 7 *Boston Herald* headline, for example, mistakenly read, "Three Are Arrested for Braintree Murders; Two Are Identified."[6] (Buda actually had escaped capture and arrest.)

Sacco and Vanzetti were held in the Bridgewater jail pending filing of formal charges. Meanwhile Stewart interrogated both men about their possible participation in the Bridgewater holdup of September 1919. Confident that Vanzetti's statements implicated him, on June 11 Stewart charged Vanzetti with that robbery attempt as well.

Boston area anarchists, along with sympathetic Wobblies and Communists, were seething as news of the arrests spread. Convinced that two innocent immigrants had been framed, anarchist newspapers took the offensive. The small newspaper *Cronaca Sovversiva*, or *Subversive Newspaper*, for example, denounced the arrests as Red Scare hysteria and ran a front-page story that read in part: "Two of our active good friends and comrades have been involved in one of those tragic, dark plots in which innocence has

POLITICAL ACTIVITIES OF VANZETTI

Vanzetti was a more committed anarchist than was Sacco. An introspective, quiet, and intellectual man, Vanzetti was a loner who described himself, according to Francis Russell in his book *Tragedy in Dedham: The Story of the Sacco and Vanzetti Case*, as "nameless in the crowd of nameless ones." Yet after his day's work selling fish, he regularly attended anarchist meetings and spoke eloquently and passionately at Sunday rallies urging local immigrants to support local labor strikes.

In 1919 Vanzetti worked as a writer for Luigi Galleani's anarchist newspaper, *Cronaca Sovversiva (Subversive Chronicle)* until May, when Galleani was deported back to Italy. One of the more vociferous flyers that Vanzetti worked on, entitled *Plain Words*, found in Russell's book, made this case for revolution:

> The powers that be make no secret of their will to stop, here in America, the world-wide spread of revolution. The powers that be must reckon that they will have to accept the fight they have provoked.
>
> A time has come when the social question's solutions can be delayed no longer; the class war is on and cannot cease but with a complete victory for the international proletariat. Do not say that we are acting cowardly because we keep in hiding, do not say it is abominable; it is a war, class war, and you are the first to wage it.
>
> There will have to be bloodshed . . . we will destroy to rid the world of your tyrannical institutions. Long live social revolution! Down with Tyranny!

all the semblance of guilt. . . . We are convinced that an attempt is being made, through the persons of Sacco and Vanzetti, to strike at all subversive elements. . . . We face a severe, a terrible test."[7]

From the moment that Sacco and Vanzetti were arrested, the panic of the Red Scare and counteraccusations of xenophobia and antiradical and anti-immigrant prejudice clouded the controversy over the guilt or innocence of the accused. Old Yankee Americans hoped the arrests, representing a hard line against subversive activity, would begin to quell civil unrest and the recent spate of violence across America. Those sympathetic to the plight of poor immigrants, however, feared what they viewed as the irrational and vengeful actions of Old Yankee Americans seeking to continue to oppress the poor. From this perspective, neither man could receive a fair trial.

While local anarchists debated defense strategies, Vanzetti was quickly brought to trial for the Bridgewater robbery. On July 1, 1920, he was found guilty and sentenced to a jail term of between twelve and fifteen years. Because he would soon be brought up on charges for the South Braintree murders, Stewart left him in the Bridgewater jail with Sacco.

On the advice of Boston's most influential anarchist, newspaper editor Carlo Tresca, Fred H. Moore, a high-profile lawyer from California, was brought in to lead the defense. Moore had

Sacco and Vanzetti hired Fred H. Moore, a high-profile labor attorney, to lead their defense. Moore had a proven record as a defense attorney in cases involving anarchists.

built his reputation successfully defending union leaders and anarchists. In Boston he immediately determined that the best hopes for acquittals rested on turning what might have been an ordinary criminal trial into a closely watched political event. On September 14, 1920, Sacco and Vanzetti were formally indicted for the South Braintree murders and moved from Bridgewater to the jail in Dedham, a small town ten miles south of Boston, where their trial was scheduled to begin on May 31, 1921. Moore had plenty of time to prepare his defense.

Shaping Public Opinion

Over the following eight months, during which time Sacco and Vanzetti remained in the Dedham jail, Moore set out to raise awareness of the case far beyond the narrow limits of Norfolk County, Massachusetts. He worked to create stirrings of sympathy for Sacco and Vanzetti throughout the United States and Europe, charging that the pair were being framed by the government. If sufficient national and international pressure could be brought to bear on influential American politicians, Moore reasoned, U.S. law enforcement agencies might be forced to reduce the charges or even drop the case altogether.

To that end, Moore circulated favorable profiles of his clients and unfavorable profiles of the prosecution. He presented the judge in the upcoming trial, Webster Thayer, as a bigot with biases against immigrants and radical politics. He also ridiculed the excess of Attorney General Palmer, who by this point in the Red Scare had rounded up and deported, without trials, several thousand immigrants who were active in the anarchist and Communist movements.

At the same time Moore did his best to portray Sacco and Vanzetti as model law-abiding workingmen respectful of the freedoms and opportunities that America had offered them. He emphasized the fact that neither man had a prior criminal record. He also encouraged Sacco's wife, Rosina, to make public appearances with their small child to reinforce Sacco's image as a family man. He minimized the two men's history of anti-American activity, including draft evasion during the war.

Sacco's wife Rosina poses for a photo in the kitchen. The defense widely circulated such images to bolster Sacco's image as a family man with a normal domestic life.

Moore's pretrial publicity blitz worked to make Sacco and Vanzetti a famous international cause. He organized public Sunday meetings in parks, solicited the support of labor unions, contacted international organizations, initiated his own private investigations, called for street marches across America in support of Sacco and Vanzetti, and distributed tens of thousands of pamphlets for the defense throughout the United States and

A crowd of workers demonstrates in New York in support of Sacco and Vanzetti. Moore encouraged workers across the United States to organize similar rallies.

beyond its borders. The campaign drew not only emotional and political support but cash—donations to the cause flowed into the Sacco and Vanzetti Defense Fund. Moore's assertive strategy transformed a little-known case into an international spectacle, attracting newsmen and radio commentators from around the world to the courtroom.

His efforts to incite community outrage may have provoked more violence. On September 16, 1920, just two days after Katzmann brought formal charges against Sacco and Vanzetti, Mario Buda, who had dropped out of sight, mysteriously resurfaced in New York City. He loaded a horse and buggy with explosives, which he detonated at the corner of Wall and Broad streets in the heart of Manhattan's financial district. The blast killed thirty, injured two hundred, and caused $2 million in property damage. Buda escaped to Italy, where he later admitted that the bomb was revenge for the prosecution of Sacco and Vanzetti.

By the opening day of the trial, the stage had been set for emotional confrontation. Anticipating a large rally of supporters, a sizable contingency of state police patrolled Dedham on horseback and motorcycles on the morning of May 31, 1921. Minutes before 9:00 A.M. police escorted the manacled Sacco and Vanzetti on their short walk from the jail to the courthouse. As the squad moved forward, hundreds of protesters lining the street and courthouse courtyard cheered their champions with encouraging shouts in both English and Italian. Many of them also carried signs bearing slogans such as "Sacco and Vanzetti Are Innocent Men—They Shall Not Be Murdered," "Libertà O Morte! [Freedom or Death!] Sacco and Vanzetti," "We Want Justice for Sacco and Vanzetti," and "Ghastly Miscarriage of Justice—The American Federation of Labor." [8]

What the newspapers were already calling the trial of the century was underway. As the two defendants and their guards stepped through the courthouse doors, the chaotic sounds and shouts of police restraining protesters outside slowly faded to the quiet and orderly atmosphere of Judge Webster Thayer's courtroom.

Chapter 2

The Prosecution:
The Case for Old
Yankee America

W HEN JUDGE THAYER gaveled open the trial in May 1921, the murders of Parmenter and Berardelli were undisputed. Legally, the only issue to be decided, and the focus of the trial, was the guilt or innocence of the defendants. Were Sacco and Vanzetti murderers or were they not?

Nevertheless, the emotionally charged Red Scare atmosphere permeated the proceeding. The case for the prosecution would be presented by Katzmann, the man who had interrogated the defendants on the night of their arrest and focused on their anarchist activities. Katzmann was a large, balding man who dressed impeccably in stylish yet conservative hand-tailored suits. In appearance, he was a typical member of Boston's patrician class. He was a graduate of Harvard University Law School, and his Bostonian accent carried identifiable upper-crust inflections. Katzmann clearly epitomized Old Yankee Americans, and they were happy to have him prosecute this case.

Judge Webster Thayer

Katzmann was pleased when it was announced that Thayer, a personal friend, would preside over the Sacco and Vanzetti case. Thayer had a reputation as a no-nonsense judge. He considered himself tough minded but fair. He was known to rule his courtroom

JUDGE WEBSTER THAYER

Sixty-four-year-old Webster Thayer had a stern look, thinning hair, a crooked nose, a face so wrinkled that he looked much older than his actual age, and he rarely smiled. Thayer had been raised in a family with long New England traditions. After graduating from college he briefly considered a professional career in major league baseball before turning to law school. Although his family had not been upper crust, he had pretensions of belonging to their ranks.

The choice of Thayer was widely applauded by mainstream America. He was an ardent supporter of Attorney General A. Mitchell Palmer as well as his raids against Red activists. Thayer was also known to express publicly his deep fear and dislike of anarchists. Even during the trial and following it, friends and enemies widely quoted him as having scorned Nicola Sacco and Bartolomeo Vanzetti as threats to America's security.

Thayer was widely denounced by American intellectuals, defense attorney Fred H. Moore, and supporters of Sacco and Vanzetti. In the opinion of Herbert B. Ehrmann, assistant defense attorney to Moore and author of the book *The Case That Will Not Die: Commonwealth vs. Sacco & Vanzetti*, "Among all the Superior Court judges in the Commonwealth, many of whom were as conscientious and fair as the lot of humanity could permit, he was the one most likely to determine upon securing a conviction."

with a heavy gavel, tolerating nothing beyond the scope of law and relevant evidence and testimony. However, although Thayer was charged with impartiality by law, his notion of impartiality was questioned from the outset. This would not be Thayer's first trial involving anarchists. In April 1920, Thayer presided over a case in which a known anarchist, Sergei Zagroff, had been acquitted of breaking certain antianarchist laws that had been enacted at the urging of Attorney General Palmer. According to an article published in the *Boston Herald*, "Judge Thayer denounced the jury for rendering the acquittal of Zagroff."[9] Thayer's criticism of the jury's verdict made him a popular champion in Old Yankee circles but an adversary among dissident groups.

It was also not the first time that Thayer had laid eyes on one of the defendants. He had presided over Vanzetti's first trial, for the December 1919 bungled payroll robbery in Bridgewater, for which Vanzetti was already serving time. Many believed that conviction foreshadowed the outcome of this trial.

Because Thayer had criticized the jury in the Zagroff acquittal and had played a role in Vanzetti's conviction in the failed Bridgewater robbery, there were calls for his removal and the appointment of another judge, perhaps one less prejudicial toward immigrant anarchists. Others argued that it was not uncommon for judges to see the same man brought to trial on different charges. There was no question that Thayer would play a pivotal role in the trial by ruling on the admissibility of evidence and by instructing the jury as to possible verdicts and their deliberations.

Tipping the Scales of Justice

Katzmann had two other, more tangible advantages over the defense. The first was the setting of the trial, a picture-perfect seat of Old Yankee traditions. Massachusetts law required the trial to be held in Norfolk County, where the murders were committed. The Norfolk County courthouse was in the city of Dedham, just a few miles from the crime scene. Dedham, a historic suburb of Boston, boasted colonial-era homes, patriotic statues, and a rich heritage dating back to the mid–seventeenth century.

Attorneys for Sacco and Vanzetti objected unsuccessfully to what they viewed as a prejudicial venue. The city stood in sharp contrast to the poor Italian-immigrant neighborhood of the defendants, and Dedham's well-to-do conservative residents had little in common with struggling newcomers to America.

This disparity was Katzmann's second advantage. Massachusetts law required that all twelve jurors and the judge be residents of Norfolk County. Defense attorney Moore, who had arrived too late to influence the selection of Thayer, was intensely concerned about jury selection. Few if any Italian citizens were likely to appear on the list of prospective jurors, and the likelihood that a juror would be sympathetic to or even open minded about the radical principles of anarchism was even more remote.

Katzmann's Strategy

Katzmann intensely wanted to win a conviction in this case. The murders of the shoe company employees were particularly brutal, at point-blank range, and completely unprovoked. In addition, Katzmann and other like-minded citizens assumed that the stolen money, none of which had been recovered, would be used to fund additional Red activities. Katzmann wanted an end, once and for all, to the anarchist violence that had plagued the nation.

Police officers guard the Norfolk County courthouse where Sacco and Vanzetti were tried. Defense attorneys argued that this was a prejudicial venue.

Katzmann developed a three-prong prosecution strategy. First, he would place the accused men at or near the crime scene. Several eyewitnesses would testify that they could identify Sacco and Vanzetti as two of the men involved in the daytime heist. Second, he would establish that one of the defendants fired one or more of the bullets killing Berardelli. Katzmann was prepared to submit as evidence ballistics reports tying the .32 caliber Colt confiscated on the night of the arrests to bullets recovered from the body of Berardelli. Third, he would expose Sacco and Vanzetti as liars as evidence of their guilt. On the night of their arrests, both men had told Katzmann a series of lies during the initial interrogation. These lies, alleged Katzmann, demonstrated what he labeled over and over again as "consciousness of guilt." This term, commonly used by attorneys, was intended to mean that the two men, conscious of their guilt in the murders of Parmenter and Berardelli, had intentionally lied to police to avoid arrest.

Vanzetti (left) and Sacco (center) sit in the prisoners' dock during their trial. Their legal proceedings lasted more than seven years.

Inside the white-walled courtroom, armed officers escorted the handcuffed Sacco and Vanzetti to the iron-bar cage where they would sit for the duration of the trial. Such a defendant cage was customary at the time. It looked like a large iron crib with chest-high sides, no top, and a door. Inside the cage was room for the defendants' chairs.

The Prosecution Begins

On May 31, 1921, as the defendants sat isolated from the press, the jury pool, and court spectators, Sheriff Samuel Capen ceremonially banged his staff and cried out, "Hear ye! Hear ye! God Save the Commonwealth of Massachusetts!" [10] With that pronouncement, Thayer took his seat on the high bench and jury selection commenced. Over the next week, counsel whittled a pool of seven hundred local citizens down to twelve through extensive questioning. The final panel was composed of twelve local men; none was a poor immigrant, yet none was a wealthy patrician either.

On June 7, 1921, assistant prosecutor Harold Williams delivered the opening statement for the prosecution. Katzmann knew that one of the keys to conviction was the positive identification of Sacco and Vanzetti at or near the crime scene. Between the time of the murders and the trial, he had interviewed thirty-four witnesses. Their accounts varied; all said that they had seen the defendants on April 15, 1920, some before the crime, others at the crime scene, and still others later in the day. Some thought they heard Italian being spoken, others thought what they heard was Spanish. Katzmann had eliminated many of the thirty-four as unreliable. But he still believed he had several witnesses who could provide damaging testimony.

Katzmann called a sequence of four witnesses who claimed they could place Vanzetti near the crime scene. The first of these, John E. Faulkner, said he saw Vanzetti get off a train at East Braintree at ten o'clock on the morning of April 15. The second, Harry E. Dolbeare, claimed to have seen Vanzetti in the backseat of a dark touring car near South Braintree Square, between ten and twelve o'clock on the morning of the murders.

Crossing guard Michael Levangie claimed to have seen Vanzetti driving a car past the South Braintree station soon after he heard shots fired. And the fourth man, railroad gate tender Austin T. Reed, testified that he saw Vanzetti get out of the front passenger seat of a car at another crossing, near Bridgewater, around 4:15 P.M. the day of the murders. None had seen Vanzetti with a gun.

Katzmann then called seven eyewitnesses who were to testify that they saw Sacco in or near South Braintree around the time of the crime. But, to Katzmann's surprise, on the witness stand a few would only say that Sacco resembled one of the bandits, but declined to make a positive identification. One of these was Bostock, the first person on the scene following the shooting. He said he was certain that the getaway car was a Buick and that the rear window was broken. He then described the two shooters as wearing dark clothes and said that one wore a cap. Bostock testified, "They appeared to be foreigners. I thought they were Italian fruit peddlers."[11] Yet, when asked if he could positively identify either Sacco or Vanzetti as the shooters, he could not. His uncertainty would be pivotal to defense arguments.

The most dramatic and potentially damaging witnesses were Mary Splaine and Lola Andrews. Splaine, a bookkeeper for the Slater and Morrill Shoe Company, positively identified Sacco as one of the shooters. So did Andrews, who had gone to the Slater and Morrill factory on April 15 to apply for a job. Splaine testified that she had about a four-second opportunity to view the shootings from her office window, eighty feet away. She said that she saw the Buick pull up to the robbery scene and then saw the shooting. She also positively identified Sacco as one of the shooters who was inside the car. She gave a detailed description of Sacco's face, the gun, and his hand holding the gun.

Andrews also identified Sacco as the man who had directed her to the factory office where she intended to apply for the job. She had gone to the shoe factory with two friends, and because none had been there before, she noticed Sacco working on a blue car and asked him for directions to the employment office. She described him and the clothes he was wearing in great detail.

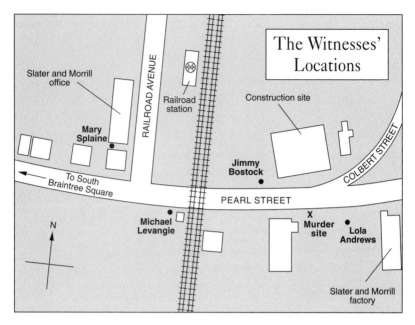

Katzmann then asked her to point out Sacco in the courtroom and she did. At that moment, Sacco stood and for the first time spoke out defiantly from the cage, "I am the man? Do you mean me? Take a good look." [12] Andrews did not respond to the outburst. Confident that his two witnesses had given credible testimony, Katzmann presented the ballistics evidence.

The Ballistics Report

The second element of the prosecution's case was to establish that at least one of the bullets in Berardelli's body came from the gun Sacco was carrying at the time of his arrest. Medical examiner George Magraph had dug four bullets out of Berardelli's body and one from Parmenter's—a sixth had apparently ricocheted after being fired and fallen harmlessly into Parmenter's pocket. Magraph identified one of the four removed from Berardelli as the fatal slug and labeled it "bullet number III."

All six bullets had been sent to a crime lab, where they were inspected and photographed. All six were determined to have been fired from a .32 caliber pistol, but one of them, bullet number III from Berardelli's body, had peculiar left-handed twist markings, or grooves, while the other five had right-handed twist markings. Twist markings indicate a bullet's direction of rotation as it exits the pistol barrel.

The ballistics technicians had fired fourteen .32 caliber test bullets from the gun confiscated from Sacco. The bullets were fired into a box filled with compressed oil-soaked sawdust to stop them without adding more scratches. The bullets were then retrieved from the sawdust and the minute scratch marks on them, incised as they exited the barrel, were compared under a microscope with the scratch marks on the bullets taken from Berardelli's body. Ballistics experts William Proctor and Charles Van Amburgh described the test results on the stand.

The prosecution first called Proctor, a police captain for sixteen years now working at the police ballistics laboratory. Katzmann asked Proctor if any of the four bullets taken from Berardelli matched any of the test-fired bullets from Sacco's pistol. Proctor expressed the opinion that one of the four, bullet number III, was fired from a .32 caliber Colt. When asked by Katzmann, "Have you

JURY SELECTION

Both Frederick Katzmann and Fred H. Moore keenly understood the significance of jury selection. The defense team hoped to find a balanced jury that might include one or two members of Italian ancestry or one or two union members who might tend to be sympathetic toward the accused. Moore automatically excused stockbrokers, bankers, and other professional men, believing their business interests might prejudice them against the two defendants, who had often participated in violent union strikes in the Boston area. At the close of June 4, all 500 prospective jurors had been questioned but only 7 selected. Thayer ordered the sheriff to find more. An additional 175 were rounded up, and late in the afternoon of June 5 the twelve jury seats were filled.

Although the final twelve jurors were all white males and generally middle class, Moore was satisfied with the mix of occupations. One juror was a former policeman, another was a photographer, and one was a farmer. Four other jurors at one time or another had been factory workers: two as machinists, one as a brick mason, and the fourth a shoemaker. None had the background or status of either of the principal attorneys or the judge.

an opinion as to whether bullet number III was fired from Mr. Sacco's Colt?"[13] Proctor answered, "My opinion is that it is consistent with being fired by that pistol."[14]

Katzmann then called Van Amburgh, an assistant in the ballistics department of the Remington Company with eight years of experience, who described the unusual left-handed markings of bullet number III. He then corroborated Proctor's conclusion that it was consistent with a bullet that had exited Sacco's gun.

This was the most damaging evidence produced during the trial. To heighten the importance of the testimony, Katzmann passed bullet number III and one of the test-fired bullets to the jurors. Each inspected the unusual left-handed markings on the two bullets and some were seen to nod in agreement with Proctor's and Van Amburgh's testimonies.

Katzmann then concluded the ballistics testimony and shifted to the third prong of his strategy. As he faced the jury, and slowly paced up and down the length of the rail separating them from the rest of the courtroom, he began to catalog the lies and inconsistencies in the stories told by the two defendants at the time of their arrests.

Lies Indicating Consciousness of Guilt

Deceptive and misleading statements, Katzmann explained to the jury, were indicative of consciousness of guilt. He then briefly defined the term to mean that Sacco and Vanzetti lied to conceal their conscious sense of guilt for the two murders. Moore, however, knowing what was coming, rose to object that the concept of consciousness of guilt did not apply in this case. His reasoning was that if the defendants had lied, they had lied to conceal anarchist connections, not murders. Unmoved, Thayer overruled Moore and instructed Katzmann to continue.

The three lies of particular interest to Katzmann concerned the whereabouts of the defendants on April 15, where they had gotten their guns, and whether or not they knew anarchists Buda and Coacci. At the time of their arrests, Sacco had told Chief of Police Stewart that he had been at work that day at the Circle-K

Shoe factory, where he had been employed for two years. Yet when prosecutors went to the shoe factory and reviewed Sacco's time card for the month of April 1920, it showed that he had been absent on April 15. Katzmann told the jury that Sacco had changed his story when confronted with this discrepancy, saying instead that he had gone that day to the Italian consulate in Boston to acquire a passport. When asked to produce the passport, Sacco said he had not received one because the lines were very long and he had left instead of waiting. The Italian consulate could find no record of his presence, nor could anyone remember seeing him there.

Vanzetti, a fish merchant, had told Stewart that he had been selling fish that day as he routinely did. Moore produced six witnesses for Vanzetti who claimed to have purchased fish from him in Plymouth, twenty-five miles from Braintree, on April 15. Their testimony, however, was impeached by the prosecution when each admitted under cross-examination that he was either a friend of Vanzetti or confused about the date he had purchased fish.

Next Katzmann turned to the defendants' accounts of where their guns came from as evidence of consciousness of guilt. When first questioned by Stewart at the Bridgewater police station, Vanzetti had said he had bought his gun at a store but could not recall any specific information beyond that. He later admitted to Katzmann that he bought the gun from a friend named Falzini for four or five dollars a few months before his arrest.

Sacco's story was similarly dubious. His initial explanation of his possession of the pistol was that he found it and took it to the nearby woods from time to time for target shooting. He had later changed his story, saying he had bought it at a store in Boston's North End, and still later, that he had bought it in the town of Milford in 1917.

Katzmann then introduced the defendants' denials about knowing Coacci and Buda, both known anarchists on Palmer's list of radicals to be deported. In fact both Sacco and Vanzetti had known them for at least three years, during which time all four had

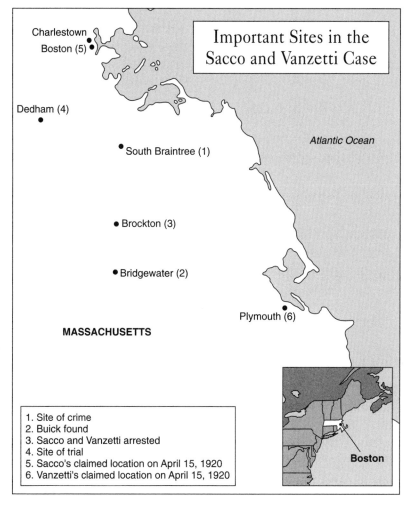

Important Sites in the Sacco and Vanzetti Case

Charlestown
Boston (5)

Dedham (4)

South Braintree (1)

Atlantic Ocean

Brockton (3)

Bridgewater (2)

Plymouth (6)

MASSACHUSETTS

1. Site of crime
2. Buick found
3. Sacco and Vanzetti arrested
4. Site of trial
5. Sacco's claimed location on April 15, 1920
6. Vanzetti's claimed location on April 15, 1920

Boston

been active in anarchist activities of various kinds throughout the Boston area. Katzmann introduced anarchist flyers containing the names of all four men announcing a meeting they had attended together in New York just months before the arrests. Yet, when the two had been specifically asked if they were anarchists or Communists by Stewart on the night of their arrest, neither man said yes.

In a move that proved controversial, Katzmann then raised the issue of the defendants' political beliefs as reason to judge them guilty. He set out to show the jury of Norfolk County citizens that Sacco and Vanzetti were unpatriotic and cowardly through a

SACCO AND VANZETTI'S FLIGHT TO MEXICO

Several historians of the Sacco and Vanzetti trial point to testimony related to the defendants' flight to Mexico to avoid the draft as both extremely damaging and clearly inadmissible. Although their flight was a violation of law, it was irrelevant to the charges of robbery and murder brought against the defendants, and, many argue, Thayer was remiss in allowing the subject to be introduced.

The prosecution used the pair's wartime record to portray the two defendants as cowardly, unpatriotic foreigners willing to take advantage of the benefits of American society yet unwilling to show their gratitude by making the same sacrifice during war required of other American men. Its effect on the jury is hard to measure, but legal analysts argue that it transformed the case. Historian Katie Sophiea writes in her article "The Sacco-Vanzetti Controversy: A Question of Prejudicial Justice," "[Prosecutor] Katzmann's opening question to Vanzetti at the trial about draft dodging changed the entire pace of the proceedings and its outcome." Roberta Strauss Feuerlicht, in her book, *Justice Crucified: The Story of Sacco and Vanzetti*, echoes Sophiea, noting, "The examination of both men about their travel to Mexico altered the trial from a mere criminal trial to a political one. Thus began the real trial of Sacco and Vanzetti."

description of their 1917 flight to Mexico to avoid induction into the army, an evasion called draft dodging.

Draft Dodging

One of Katzmann's intentions was to sway the emotions of the jury against the defendants by portraying them as Reds at odds with American law and traditions. As an example of their unwillingness to conform to the nation that had magnanimously provided them a new home, Katzmann chose to attack their refusal to join the army during World War I. This was an especially volatile issue just two years after the end of the war and at the time of the Red Scare.

Although a record of draft evasion had no bearing on the murders of Parmenter and Berardelli, Katzmann reminded the jurors that the two immigrants had obeyed the call of the anarchist leader Luigi Galleani to flaunt the law requiring them to register for the draft and that they had turned their backs on the country that had taken them in.

The first question Katzmann asked Vanzetti was, "So you left Plymouth, Mr. Vanzetti, in May 1917, to dodge the draft, did you?"[15] Vanzetti admitted he had done so. Katzmann continued the same line of questioning when Vanzetti was recalled to the stand days later. Katzmann hammered the question again, "When this country was at war, you ran away so you would not have to fight as a soldier? Is that true?"[16] Vanzetti again said it was true.

Sacco was next to take the witness stand. Katzmann immediately ripped into him for fleeing to Mexico. His line of questioning, however, was slightly different. Sacco's flight meant leaving

Nicola Sacco poses with his wife Rosina and son Dante in a 1927 photo. The prosecution characterized Sacco as a man who had deserted his family.

his wife and child. Katzmann began, "Did you run away to Mexico to avoid being a soldier for this country that you loved?" [17] Sacco said he had. Katzmann's questioning became more personal: "And is that your idea of showing love for your wife that when she needed you you ran away from her?" [18] At that point, Moore objected and Thayer ended the questioning. Nonetheless, Katzmann had successfully given the jury an impression of the defendants as cowardly and unappreciative of America and of Sacco as a deserting husband and father.

On June 21, 1921, Katzmann rested the case for the prosecution. He was pleased with his performance. He believed that he and his team had presented sufficient evidence to convince the jury that the defendants were the men responsible for the murders. Moore, however, who would now have his opportunity to present the case for the defense, was equally confident that Katzmann had fallen short of the mark.

Chapter 3

The Defense: Blaming Red Scare Hysteria

T HE TIMING OF the trial could not have been worse for the two Italian immigrants. Self-confessed anarchists, participants in labor strikes, and draft dodgers from World War I, Sacco and Vanzetti were viewed with suspicion and loathing and portrayed in the media and in the court of public opinion as dangerously un-American. According to some court observers, the two men never stood a chance.

Defense attorney Moore, however, had another view. He had been tirelessly working on the case for close to a year and believed he could discredit the testimony and evidence brought by the prosecution. Furthermore, and of greater importance, Moore believed he could convince the jurors that the trial was politically motivated as part of the Red Scare hysteria still sweeping America. He knew it would be an uphill battle but believed the battle could be won.

Defender of Radical Politics

From the start Moore was at odds with New England traditions and sensibilities. He appeared in court with his trademark long hair combed straight back from his forehead. He was frequently seen casually walking the streets of Dedham in sandals and a broad-brimmed cowboy hat—not the sort of attire Old Yankee Americans expected from respectable members of the legal community.

The defense attorney's politics were also at odds with local conservatives. Prior to coming to Dedham, all his cases, both well known and obscure, had been in defense of Red activists. He was known as a champion of the Wobblies and other militant groups, and although respected, he was roughly characterized by historian Francis Russell as an attorney who "drifted from one labor fight to another, taking on the hopeless, desperate cases that could not afford better-known lawyers." [19]

Moore's courtroom reputation was that of a fiery orator. Many prosecutors and judges were offended by his aggressive outbursts yet respected their effectiveness. He also had a reputation as a thorough and tireless worker and a careful observer of jurors who could tailor comments and speeches to specific jurors and appeal to their individual personalities.

FRED H. MOORE

Fred H. Moore grew up in a respectable middle-class family in Seattle, Washington, and graduated from the University of Washington Law School in 1913. Moore's political leanings while in college were decidedly conservative, so it was no surprise to anyone that his first job was representing one of Washington's largest corporations, the railroad.

Following two years practicing law in Seattle, Moore took a more lucrative and promising job in Los Angeles, where he demonstrated his brilliance and eagerness to work his way up the corporate ladder. One day when a friend in San Diego was arrested at an Industrial Workers of the World (IWW) rally, Moore packed a suitcase, told his secretary he would soon return, and headed to San Diego.

Moore successfully defended his friend but never returned to his Los Angeles law firm. From that time on he made a career of traveling from town to town defending IWW workers arrested for a variety of labor law violations. In 1919 Moore successfully defended an IWW striker accused of bombing the house of a Standard Oil official. Following this case, Moore was introduced to Carlo Tresca, who in 1920 asked him to lead the defense of Nicola Sacco and Bartolomeo Vanzetti.

Francis Russell quotes journalist Eugene Lyons's assessment of Moore in his book, *Tragedy in Dedham: The Story of the Sacco and Vanzetti Case:* "He was at heart an artist. There is some truth to the charge that he subordinated the literal needs of legalistic procedure to the larger needs of the case as a symbol of class struggle. If he had not done so, Sacco and Vanzetti would have been dead six years earlier."

Like Katzmann, Moore had developed a three-pronged strategy. He would challenge the credibility of the witnesses presented by the prosecution, provide contradicting ballistics testimony, and show that the lies told by Sacco and Vanzetti on the night of their arrests were entirely unrelated to the murders of Parmenter and Berardelli.

Moore determined that from the outset he would have Sacco and Vanzetti frankly acknowledge their political activity in court and establish that their arrest and prosecution stemmed from their radical activities. He would try to expose what he and many others believed to be the prosecution's hidden motive: a desire to aid government authorities in suppressing the Italian anarchist movement to which Sacco and Vanzetti belonged.

Confused Witnesses

Aided by an associate, Jeremiah J. McAnarney, Moore began by recalling all witnesses presented by the prosecution to cast doubt on their identification of either Sacco or Vanzetti as participants in the crime. It was crucial to discredit the testimony of Splaine and Andrews in particular because both had positively identified Sacco as one of the shooters.

Splaine was called to the stand first. McAnarney asked Splaine if Sacco was the man she saw fire the pistol from the Buick, which had been her earlier testimony. Shocking the courtroom, she answered that she had not seen Sacco fire anything. McAnarney immediately pointed out her contradiction and had the court reporter reread her testimony. Her response was that her previous identification was not what she had really meant to say. McAnarney then pressed his advantage by questioning whether it was possible for her to have seen any detail at all in four seconds from eighty feet down the street.

Arguing that her testimony was weak, he then asked if she had gone to the police station following the arrests to identify Sacco. She said that she had, on three different occasions. With that, McAnarney wheeled around and directly addressed the jurors: "Gentlemen, that description, is built . . . from top to bottom, not from what she saw from the window but from what she saw in the police station. You know it. Gentlemen, are you going to use that kind of testimony to take a human life?" [20]

The other star eyewitness for the prosecution, Andrews, was next. Like Splaine, Andrews had identified Sacco in jail in March 1921. McAnarney now asked her to recall basic observations: What was Sacco wearing at the time and was he alone in the cell? Her response to both questions was that she could not remember. McAnarney proceeded to discredit all her previous testimony, including remarkably detailed descriptions of Sacco and his clothing on the day of the murder in April 1920. He turned to the jury box and argued that if she did not know the answers to simple questions based on her visit to the jail three months earlier, she could not be trusted to know what she had seen a full year earlier.

Then McAnarney called Andrews's two friends who had accompanied her to the shoe company on the day of the murders. He asked each if Andrews had spoken with Sacco or anyone who looked like him. Neither could recall any such conversation, nor did either remember seeing Sacco.

Following examinations of these four witnesses, McAnarney pointed out that neither Splaine nor Andrews had identified Sacco until well after his arrest, and that no witness had been required to pick Sacco out of a lineup, a standard procedure. But most damaging to the prosecution's case at this point was the fact that none of these five—not Faulkner, Dolbeare, Levangie, Reed, or Bostock, all of whom were close to the crime scene—were able to identify either defendant in the courtroom.

Furthermore, no one claimed to have seen Vanzetti at the murder scene. A defense witness testified that Levangie said a few minutes after the shooting that it would be hard to identify the man he had seen driving the car. Another witness testified that Levangie told him that he saw no one, while a third witness said Levangie initially said the driver was light haired, yet as all in the court could see, Vanzetti was dark haired.

For each prosecution witness who placed one of the defendants in South Braintree or near the crime scene, the defense was

Sacco (right) and Vanzetti stand in handcuffs outside the courthouse. Moore's defense rested on the premise that his clients were victims of Red Scare hysteria.

able to produce a witness who contradicted that testimony by placing them elsewhere or by raising serious doubts about witness credibility. Most witnesses admitted on cross-examination that the startling confusion caused by the gunshots, their distance from the murders, and the year separating the crime from the trial made positive identification difficult.

Moore sensed that the conflicting and confused testimony by witnesses had been effective. Knowing that he had to be even more convincing to undermine the ballistics testimony, he moved on to challenge the key evidence: bullet number III.

Contradictory Ballistics Experts

Moore first called Proctor, the man who associated bullet number III with Sacco's pistol, to the stand. Moore's tactic was not to dispute the markings but rather to raise doubts about Proctor's ballistics expertise. He asked the witness if he knew the maximum pressure, pounds per square inch, generated when the bullet was fired. Proctor responded, "I don't know anything along that line. My experience is in examining, measuring, and comparing bullets." [21]

Moore then stepped forward and announced that he would present two more witnesses to the test shootings of the guns confiscated from Sacco and Vanzetti—James Burns and J. Henry

THE SACCO AND VANZETTI DEFENSE FUND

Defense attorney Fred H. Moore's strategy of trying the case in the court of public opinion was expensive and time-consuming. To pay the high costs of publicity, printing, and protest organization, Moore conceived the idea of the Sacco and Vanzetti Legal Defense Fund.

Much of the money was raised through painstaking solicitation in poor working-class immigrant neighborhoods, collected twenty-five and fifty cents at a time. Donations also flowed in from European and South American cities in envelopes stuffed with foreign currencies.

Groups such as the New England Civil Liberties Union soon joined the fund-raising effort. Its supporters received a letter declaring that the evidence against Sacco and Vanzetti was unsubstantial and, according to Douglas Linder's article "The Trial of Sacco and Vanzetti," that they were being prosecuted merely because they were "foreigners and active and influential radicals."

A related organization, the Sacco and Vanzetti Defense Committee, was also successful in pressuring the jury and politicians during the trial and appeals process. The committee was able to call upon thousands of grassroots supporters to appear at the courthouse to voice their support for Sacco and Vanzetti as jurors and other participants entered and departed. Carrying signs, they pleaded their case for the two accused men. They also formed groups to write protest letters to politicians and newspapers and to argue their case.

Fitzgerald. Burns testified that he had spent thirty years as a ballistics engineer working for the U.S. Cartridge Factory. He agreed that bullet number III could have been fired from Sacco's .32 caliber Colt but quickly added that it might just as likely have come from any .32 caliber pistol. Moore then handed six of the test-fired bullets along with bullet number III to Burns and asked, "Do these bullets have the same irregularities shown on bullet number III?" [22] "Not in my opinion," answered Burns, "Bullet number III doesn't compare at all with these six." [23] Moore then noted to the jury that this testimony contradicted the testimony of the ballistics witnesses presented by the prosecution.

Fitzgerald then took the stand and identified himself as a ballistics expert with twenty-eight years of experience presently employed by the Colt firearms company—the company that had manufactured Sacco's gun. When asked to describe bullet number III, he replied, "Number III was not fired from the Sacco's pistol. I can see no pitting or marks on bullet number III that would correspond with a bullet coming from his gun." [24] Just as had been the case with the eyewitnesses to the murders, the expert ballistics witnesses appeared to at least neutralize each other and perhaps raise serious doubt in the minds of the jurors.

Reasonable Explanations for the Defendants' Lies

Moore next confidently directed his attention to the jury to confront the lies his clients told on the night they were arrested. He intended to persuade the jury that indeed they had lied, but not to cover up the shootings.

The attorney made the case that when his clients were arrested, initially for carrying concealed weapons, neither man was informed of the reason for his arrest. As Sacco and Vanzetti were anarchists who had participated in union strikes and antigovernment demonstrations, both had every reason to assume their arrests were part of Palmer's continuing raids on Reds. Moore argued that Sacco and Vanzetti lied to cover up their illegal political activities, not murders.

To support this argument, Moore pointed to the death of a leading anarchist, Andrea Salsedo, just two days before the arrest of Sacco and Vanzetti. Salsedo had been found dead on a sidewalk below FBI offices where he was being held for questioning in a bombing. Whether he was pushed or jumped no one knew, but in a climate of paranoia, anarchists throughout New England feared others in FBI custody might come to the same end. Because of the Salsedo incident, Moore continued, his anarchist clients concocted spur-of-the-moment, admittedly transparent lies, fearing the truth about their political involvement could mean their own violent death at government hands.

For these reasons, Moore continued, the concept of consciousness of guilt, which he had vehemently opposed at the outset of the trial, simply did not apply. He explained that the defendants had gone to the Elm Street Garage with Coacci and Buda to pick up the car so they could load it with illegal anarchist literature they had been warned to dispose of, drive it to a remote place, and dump it. Sacco and Vanzetti knew that possessing and distributing Red literature, which they admitted they had done, might cause their arrest and deportation.

To highlight this position, McAnarney called Vanzetti to the stand and asked him, "Why did you not tell Mr. Stewart the truth that night when he arrested you and talked to you at the station?"[25] Vanzetti answered, "I was scared to give the names of my friends as I know that almost all of them have some books and newspapers in their houses by which the authority might arrest them and deport them."[26]

The defense counsel then raised the issue of avoiding induction in the army. Vanzetti testified that he had feared the authorities might learn that he had fled to Mexico to avoid being drafted in 1917. Flight to avoid the draft was considered a reprehensible crime during the war, and indeed large numbers of Communists and anarchists were vilified for refusing to serve. However, as McAnarney reiterated, this was a far less serious crime than murder.

With that, the defense rested its case. Moore had met his objectives of countering all of the prosecution evidence. At

this point in trial procedure, each side moved to present closing arguments.

The Defense's Summation: Treat Them as Your Brother

On July 13, Moore stepped forward to deliver the summation for
the defense. To save his clients from the electric chair, he focused
on two factors that had been at the heart of his case: contradictory
testimony and his clients' fears of government reprisals for their
militant political activities.

*Heavily guarded, Sacco and Vanzetti are escorted from prison on the final day of
their trial. On the charge of first-degree murder, the jury returned a guilty verdict.*

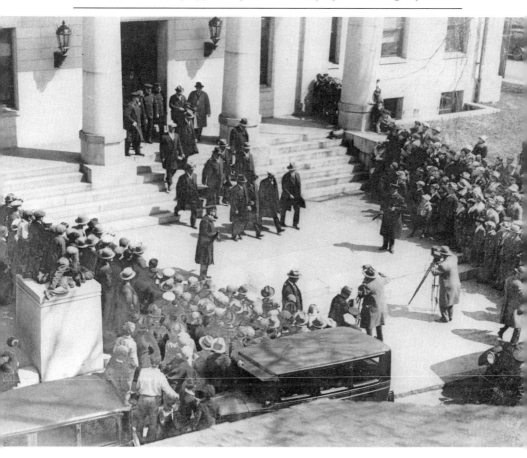

Moore began by reviewing the testimony of key witnesses. His intent was to remind the jurors of the contradictory testimony given by witnesses for the prosecution and conflicting testimony among expert witnesses, especially regarding the ballistics evidence. He reminded the jurors that Bostock, the first person to the crime scene, could not identify either Sacco or Vanzetti. Moore characterized Bostock as "a plain, solid, substantial type of American citizen who refused to make an identification." [27] He then recounted testimony by other witnesses such as Splaine and Andrews, both of whom he believed had been discredited by questionable testimony or contradicted by other witnesses.

THE CAP

Many incidental details of the South Braintree murders emerged during the trial testimony. One piece of circumstantial evidence particularly captured the attention of the court and the public: a cap found at the crime scene by Jimmy Bostock. The cap was a dark cloth men's cap with a torn hole in the back. During pretrial investigations by both sides, it was revealed that Nicola Sacco often wore such a cap.

The prosecution spent considerable time trying to tie Sacco to the cap, which would then tie him to the crime scene. Three full days of testimony were devoted to it. Several of Sacco's coworkers were called to look at the cap and testify as to whether or not it belonged to Sacco. All said that he did wear such a cap but none could identify it with certainty. As one witness pointed out, at that time thousands of men wore similar dark cloth caps.

The tear in the back, however, was not common to most caps. Sacco's supervisor at the Circle-K Shoe Company testified that Sacco often hung his hat on a nail when he came to work. Prosecutors saw that as evidence that the cap was his. Yet the supervisor could not identify it as belonging to Sacco, and it was later revealed that the hole had been inadvertently made by Braintree's chief of police.

When Sacco was asked to identify the cap, he insisted that it was not his and that in fact it was too small for his head. Fred H. Moore then asked him to try it on. A noticeable chuckle ran through the courtroom as all recognized that the hat indeed did not fit. The *Boston Herald* reported, "It stuck on the top of his head and he turned with a satisfied air to let the jury see." A cartoon in the *New York Times* mocked the comical moment by depicting Sacco with a cap the size of a teacup perched atop his head.

Then Moore reviewed the contradictory ballistics testimony, which he knew was critical to the case. He reread aloud much of the trial transcript of the ballistics testimony for the defense, and emphasized these men had more experience studying guns and bullets than the two witnesses for the prosecution. He also reminded the jury that Burns and Fitzgerald had concluded that bullet number III was not fired by Sacco's gun.

Finally, McAnarney closed with a plea for compassion for two immigrant Italians who spoke English badly, who looked "foreign," and who embraced a radical political philosophy. He asked for fairness: "I want every man of this panel to treat these two defendants as if they were your own individual brother. Take this as a test. . . . They came to this world by the same power that created you, and may each go from this world by the same power that takes you. I thank you, gentlemen." [28]

The Prosecution's Summation: "Stand Together, You Men of Norfolk"

The next morning it was Katzmann's turn. His closing argument was rigorously organized. He led the jurors on a step-by-step reenactment of the previous five weeks of testimony and evidence. Katzmann too highlighted the testimony of witnesses who had provided damaging evidence linking Sacco and Vanzetti to the murder scene.

Then, approaching the jury box, he dramatically produced bullet number III, the test-fired bullets, and a magnifying glass. "Determine the facts for yourselves," he said as he handed all the items to the first juror. "Take the glass, gentlemen, and examine them for yourselves. If you choose, take the word of nobody. Can there be a fairer test?" [29] One by one, each juror examined the critical bullet number III with the others.

Katzmann appealed to the jurors to conclude that, based on the evidence, Sacco was definitely one of the shooters in the murders of Parmenter and Berardelli. Vanzetti, Katzmann argued, was in the Buick getaway car but not a shooter; nonetheless, under Massachusetts law, an accomplice to a murder is just as culpable as those who fire the shots, and the jury was likewise bound to find Vanzetti guilty.

Then Katzmann raised the two highly subjective and volatile topics of the defendants' consciousness of guilt and anti-American political behavior. He dismissed the defense argument that Sacco and Vanzetti had told a series of lies because they feared being arrested for possessing illegal anarchist publications and repeated his charge that running away to Mexico and leaving behind, in Sacco's case, a wife and child to fend for themselves was clear indication of bad character.

Nearing the end of his allotted six hours, Katzmann made one last emotional appeal to the patriotism of the jury. "It is for you to say if they are guilty and you are done. Gentlemen of the jury, do your duty. Do it like men. Stand together, you men of Norfolk." [30]

The next morning, July 14, 1921, Thayer delivered his deliberation instructions to the jury. He reviewed several points of law and then issued this admonition:

> Let your eyes be blinded to every ray of sympathy or prejudice but let them ever be willing to receive the beautiful sunshine of truth, of reason, and sound judgment, and let your ears be deaf to every sound of public opinion or public clamor, if there be any, either in favor of or against these defendants. [31]

He then dismissed the court for lunch to reconvene at 2:30. At 3:00, following roll taking, he sent the jurors to the jury room to deliberate the fate of the defendants. At 7:30 that evening, just four and a half hours after the jury withdrew, the court clerk scrambled about the courthouse alerting everyone that a verdict had been reached.

"Your Honor, We Have a Verdict"

All hastily reconvened in Thayer's courtroom, and the court clerk called out, "Your honor, we have a verdict." [32] He then asked Sacco and Vanzetti to stand and face the jury foreman. Turning to the foreman, Walter Ripley, the clerk then asked, "What say you, Mr. Foreman, are the prisoners at the bar guilty or not guilty?" "Guilty" came the reply. "Guilty of murder in the first degree and upon each indictment?" "Yes sir," [33] was the foreman's response.

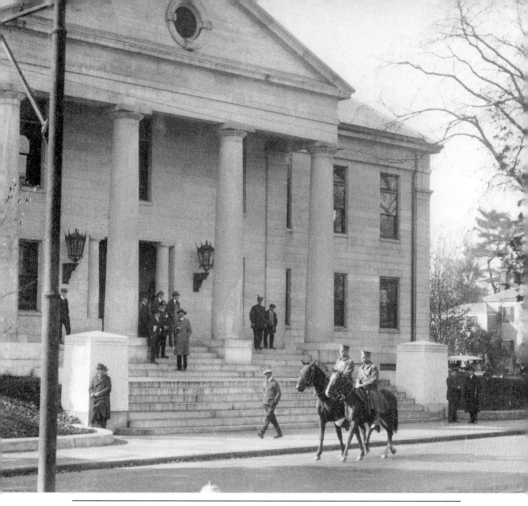

Police officers on horseback patrol the entrance to the courthouse during a motion for a new trial. The defense team filed eight separate motions for a new trial, all of which were denied.

The clerk then polled the jury, asking each juror individually if this was the verdict each had intended. Following each juror's affirmation of the verdict, Thayer thanked the jurors for their work and sent them home. The final entry in the official trial transcript is Thayer's closing words, "The Court will now adjourn."[34]

But Vanzetti was not ready to adjourn. Suddenly his voice rang through the courtroom: "Sono innocente"[35] ("I am innocent!"). Sacco's wife, Rosina, pushed her way through a ring of policemen and clung to her husband, weeping. Moore tried to pull her away, and finally a policeman escorted her from the courtroom. Then it was Sacco's turn. In broken English he shouted, "They kill an innocent men." [36] Several jurors exiting the jury box looked back but kept moving. Sacco shouted a second time, "Don't forget, two innocent men they kill!" [37]

Although the formal sentence would not be imposed by Thayer until April 9, 1927, following the end of the appeals process, everyone in the courthouse understood that barring a successful appeal for a new trial, Sacco and Vanzetti would very likely be executed for the murders. Sacco was returned to the Dedham County jail during the appeals process, but Vanzetti was sent to Charlestown State Prison, just across the Charles River from Boston.

The guilty verdict marked the end of the trial and the beginning of the struggle to keep the convicted men from the electric chair. The job of the defense team was not over. Massachusetts law provided the defense ample time to file appeals for a new trial, should they choose to do so. Winning a new trial depended upon being able to demonstrate that the trial had been flawed by intentional deception, misconduct, or improper jury instructions by the judge, or on finding new, convincing evidence that might exonerate the defendants.

Chapter 4

The Fight to Escape the Electric Chair

O VER THE NEXT six years, attorneys for Sacco and Vanzetti filed eight motions requesting a new trial, on a variety of grounds. Some argued that witnesses were not credible or that testimony had been coerced or since retracted; others alleged jury misconduct or introduced new evidence that potentially exonerated the condemned men. While these motions dragged on through the courts, the defense team doggedly continued the publicity blitz aimed at keeping Sacco and Vanzetti in the public eye and building their image as victims of injustice. Perhaps, according to Fred Moore's strategy, national and international protest might force the governor of Massachusetts to intercede and pardon the shoemaker and the fish peddler if legal maneuvers failed.

The primary, and most controversial, obstacle in the way of each motion proved to be Judge Webster Thayer. Massachusetts law required Thayer, as presiding judge in the case, to review and pass judgment on all legal motions for a new trial. This meant that a judge whom many accused of judicial prejudice was allowed to rule on whether the trial proceedings had been prejudiced, which many saw as a clear conflict of interest. The law did allow Thayer's rulings to be further appealed to the Massachusetts Supreme Court, which could overrule Thayer and grant a new trial if it determined there was cause to do so.

The first motion sent to Thayer's desk was standard and expected, filed in November 1921. It argued that the evidence presented was insufficient to warrant a guilty verdict. Thayer used few words in his rejection, saying in effect that the jury had weighed sufficient evidence and acted in a responsible manner. Even before this appeal was denied, however, Moore stumbled on information suggesting that the conduct of Walter Ripley, the jury foreman, was anything but responsible, prompting an immediate supplemental motion for a new trial.

Jury Misconduct

In the so-called Ripley motion, also filed in November 1921, Moore alleged two separate incidents of misconduct on the part of Ripley that were sufficient to warrant a new trial. The first and more serious charge was based on the allegation that Ripley carried in his pocket throughout much of the trial three of his own .38 caliber bullets, like those found in Vanzetti's revolver when he was arrested. Moore considered this both odd and a serious violation of conduct, because the law only allowed evidence formally presented in the courtroom to be considered by the jury when arriving at their decision. Having these bullets, without the knowledge of the judge, Moore argued, may have prejudiced Ripley and other jurors who saw them.

The second alleged incident of misconduct actually occurred prior to jury selection. Defense attorneys learned that an old friend of Ripley's, William Daly, encountered Ripley on his way to the courthouse when he was first summoned for jury duty. Daly testified that, in response to his own comment that the men were probably innocent, Ripley had said, "Damn them, they ought to hang them anyway." [38] Such bias, argued the defense attorneys, ought to have disqualified Ripley from the jury because Thayer specifically excused all prospective jurors who held a preconceived opinion about the innocence or guilt of the accused. Clearly, argued Moore, his off-the-cuff comment to Daly indicated a preconceived opinion of guilt.

In his rejection of this motion, Thayer noted the irregularity of Ripley carrying the three bullets but concluded that no evidence had been presented indicating that this had influenced Ripley or any other juror in any way. Thayer did not refer to Daly's testimony. Subsequent appeal of Thayer's ruling was hampered because Ripley himself could not be questioned directly—by the time the motion was rejected, he had died.

Sudden friction between Moore and Sacco surfaced in April 1923, when Moore angered Sacco by committing him to the Bridgewater Hospital for the Criminally Insane for treatment of severe depression. While in the hospital, Sacco asked Moore to withdraw from the case, complaining that he was more concerned with his own career and fund-raising than with his clients. Moore complied, removing himself as counsel for both defendants.

SACCO FIRES MOORE

Tension between Sacco and Vanzetti and their attorney flared on occasion, justified or not. The final rift occurred in spring 1923, while Sacco was confined to the Bridgewater State Hospital for the Criminally Insane while suffering from depression. During his brief stay, he composed a letter to Moore, firing him. The gist of Sacco's complaint was that Moore was a deceptive manipulator who had made a lot of money on the trial at his clients' expense. The unpolished letter and Moore's curt response is found in Francis Russell's book, *Sacco & Vanzetti: The Case Resolved:*

> Maney [Many] time you have been deluder [deluding] and abuse . . . but I want you to stop no[w] and if you please get out of my case, because you know that you are the obstacle of the case. . . . Of course it is pretty hard to refuse such sweet pay that [h]as come to you right along in this big game. Another word, if this were not the truth, you would quit this job for a long time. . . . I know that you are the one that brings in the mud [lies] in Sacco-Vanzetti case. Anyhow, whatever you do if you do not intend to get out of my case, remember this, that by September the first I want my case a finish. . . . So please tell me, what you waiting for? Do you wait till I hang myself. That's what you wish? Lett me tal you right now don't be illuse [disillusion] yourself, I would not be surprised if someone will find you some morning hanging on lamppost.
>
> Your implacable enemy now and forever, Nick Sacco.

Moore responded with the following short letter to Sacco: "Dear Mr. Sacco, enclosed you will find a copy of my withdrawal as your counsel, filed today. I wish you every possible success in your battle for justice."

The attorney who took his place, William G. Thompson, focused on the evidence that remained the most damaging to Sacco and Vanzetti's case, bullet number III. In a November 1923 motion, Thompson charged that William Proctor, one of the ballistics experts for the prosecution, had provided intentionally misleading testimony.

William G. Thompson (right) took over the defense team after Sacco and Vanzetti dismissed Fred Moore in 1923.

Bullet Number III Revisited

When Katzmann asked Proctor on the witness stand whether bullet number III had been fired by Sacco's gun, Proctor had avoided a direct yes-or-no answer. Instead he answered, "My opinion is that it is consistent with being fired by that pistol."[39] Two years after the trial, Thompson interviewed Proctor and asked him specifically why he had phrased his answer in those exact words. The answer was startling.

Proctor swore in an affidavit that prior to his court appearance, Katzmann had repeatedly discussed with him how best to ask and answer the questions about bullet number III. Proctor said that he had told Katzmann that if he were directly asked whether that bullet positively came from Sacco's gun, he would have been obliged to say no. Proctor added it was still his opinion that bullet number III passed through some Colt automatic pistol, but not necessarily through Sacco's Colt.

Katzmann was required to respond to the allegation that he had coached Proctor regarding the phrasing of the question and the answer. Katzmann denied any such thing had occurred. He went on to point out that Moore, who was the lead attorney at the time, had ample opportunity to question Proctor himself and rephrase the question if he had wished.

Thayer rejected the Proctor motion as he rejected all others. In his opinion, Katzmann and his staff had acted with the highest standards of personal conduct and he could not find sufficient reason to require a second trial. The Massachusetts Supreme Court concurred, noting, "Neither the district attorney nor his assistants intentionally solicited an ambiguous answer to the questions under consideration for the purpose of obtaining a conviction."[40]

At this point, it seemed Sacco and Vanzetti were running out of appeals, and thus running out of time. Then, on November 18, 1925, their battle to escape the electric chair took a more positive, albeit bizarre turn when a convict in the Dedham jail, where Sacco was held, secretly passed him a note.

The Jailhouse Confession

A question posed by many people following the trial and the appeals process was, If Sacco and Vanzetti did not commit the murders, then who did? According to many who supported their innocence, a local Boston group of thugs called the Morelli gang, implicated in a string of robberies, was a prime suspect.

In 1925, as Sacco and Vanzetti awaited word on the bullet number III appeal, a young Portuguese immigrant named Celestino F. Madeiros awaited his own appeal of his murder conviction. From his Dedham jail cell he sent Sacco the following note, slipped into a magazine and delivered by an inmate messenger: "I hear by confess to being in the South Braintree shoe company crime and Sacco and Vanzetti was not in said crime. CELESTINO F. MADEIROS." [41]

Attorneys for Sacco and Vanzetti read the letter and immediately obtained a sworn affidavit from Madeiros detailing his recollection of the South Braintree robbery. In his testimony, he recounted the events of April 15, including details about the time of the crime, the car—a Buick, a pistol, money in a black bag, shots fired, and the first names of the robbers. He specifically refused, however, to give their last names. On May 26, 1926, with this document in hand, attorneys filed yet another motion with Thayer for a new trial.

Defense attorneys provided three compelling reasons why it made more sense to consider the Morelli gang the true culprits. First, they asserted, the robbery was a professional job that amateurs like Sacco and Vanzetti could not have pulled off. Second, the Morelli gang had a clear motive for the robbery —robbery was their business—and better ways to hide the money, none of which had been recovered. And third, it would explain the source of all six bullets found in the two dead men rather than just bullet number III because, attorneys argued, the Morelli gang fired several guns in the holdup.

Thayer, however, dismissed Madeiros's admission of guilt as the words of "A crook, a thief, a robber, a liar, a rum-runner . . . and a man who has been convicted and sentenced to death for murder." [42] Besides noting Madeiros's lengthy criminal record, Thayer also noted a few inaccuracies in his story. One was his claim to have stolen a black bag of money, which in fact had been

SACCO'S DEATH SENTENCE STATEMENT

Following Judge Thayer's pronouncement of the death sentence on April 9, 1927, Sacco and Vanzetti were given the opportunity to address the court. The following is an excerpt from Sacco's statement, criticizing Thayer and arguing that his death is a political decision, not a legal one. The full text can be found on the Web site School of Law, University of Missouri–Kansas City.

> I am no orator. I never knew, never heard, even read in history anything so cruel as this Court. After years prosecuting they still consider us guilty. I know the sentence will be between two classes, the oppressed class and the rich class, and there will be always collision between one and the other. We fraternize the people with the books, with the literature. You persecute the people, tyrannize them and kill them. We try the education of people always. You try to put a path between us and some other nationality that hates each other. That is why I am here today on this bench, for having been of the oppressed class. Well, you are the oppressor. You know it, Judge Thayer.
>
> I would like to tell all my life, but what is the use? You forget all this population that has been with us for seven years, to sympathize and give us all their energy and all their kindness. You do not care for them. Among that peoples and the comrades and the working class there is a big legion of intellectual people which have been with us for seven years, to not commit the iniquitous sentence, but still the Court goes ahead.
>
> And I want to thank you all, you peoples, my comrades who have been with me for seven years, with the Sacco Vanzetti case, and I will give my friend a chance. I forget one thing which my comrade remember me. As I said before, Judge Thayer know all my life, and he know that I am never guilty, never—not yesterday, nor today, nor forever.

two metal boxes of money, and a second was his time line, which did not place him at the crime scene at three o'clock in the afternoon. Equally troublesome was his refusal to provide the last names of the gang members.

At this point in the appeal process, any revelation of new evidence justifying a new trial seemed increasingly unlikely. The public, which had closely followed the trial and appeals, sensed the end was near.

The Lowell Committee

After six years of unsuccessful appeals, the prospect of imminent executions fueled the national and international outcry against what many perceived to be a frameup. Stepped-up agitation on Sacco and Vanzetti's behalf by intellectuals, radicals, workers, immigrants, and even some mainstream Americans kept the case on the front pages of many newspapers. Demonstrators in many of America's largest cities and in several foreign cities took to the streets to protest the trial and sentences as biased and inhumane.

Public pressure combined with influential behind-the-scenes intervention finally persuaded the governor of Massachusetts, Alvan T. Fuller, to consider the question of executive clemency for the two men. Executive clemency would set Sacco and Vanzetti free or, at a minimum, commute the death sentence to life in prison.

Massachusetts governor Alvan T. Fuller appointed the Lowell Committee to review the Sacco and Vanzetti case. The committee upheld the guilty verdict.

Rather than assume full responsibility for such a controversial decision, Fuller appointed an advisory committee, called the Lowell Committee because its most prominent member was A. Lawrence Lowell, president of Harvard University. The committee was asked to review all court testimony to determine whether any justification could be found for reversing the finding of the jury seven years earlier.

On July 27, 1927, while Sacco and Vanzetti sat on death row, the Lowell Committee returned its findings. The committee concluded that the trial and judicial process had been fundamentally fair and that clemency was not warranted. In a short summary, the committee stated:

> On these grounds the Committee is of opinion that Sacco was guilty beyond reasonable doubt of the murder at South Braintree. In reaching this conclusion they are aware that it involves a disbelief in the evidence of his alibi at Boston, but in view of all the evidence they do not believe he was there [Boston] that day. . . . On the whole, we are of opinion that Vanzetti also was guilty beyond reasonable doubt. . . . It has been argued that a crime of this kind must have been committed by professionals, and it is for well-known criminal gangs that one must look; but to the Committee this crime does not seem to bear the marks of professionals, but of men inexpert in such crimes. [43]

Rather than extinguish questions about the unfairness of the trial, however, the report only fueled more controversy. Harvard University, because of Lowell's role, became stigmatized, in the words of one of its alumni, as "Hangman's House. . . . Not every wop [Italian] has the switch to the electric chair thrown by the president of Harvard." [44]

The Felix Frankfurter Article

In August 1927, as the end drew near, protesters expressed their outrage on both sides of the Atlantic. Everyone understood that the Lowell findings had been the last opportunity to avert the

POLICE BRACE FOR RIOTS

Police throughout the United States braced for riots the day before the execution. None was more worried than Boston's police force. To protect city residents and property, officers broke up an angry crowd of nearly five hundred Italians in the north end of the city. More than one thousand local drivers intentionally blocked Main Street while honking horns in protest.

Charlestown prison was also on full alert. Machine guns, tear-gas bombs, pistols, and riot guns were at the ready as five hundred state police assisted prison guards in preparing for a possible assault on the prison. At eleven o'clock at night, just one hour before the executions, mounted policemen charged a crowd of several thousand that gathered just outside the roped-off area surrounding the jail.

This bizarre atmosphere was heightened by motion-picture photographers whose flaming torches illuminated mounted police with a ghostly flicker that cast their silhouettes against the prison walls. The south and west walls of the prison were lined with machine guns and searchlights at twenty-yard intervals. Across some railroad tracks, patrol boats could be seen moving slowly up and down the river, each equipped with flares and searchlights that scanned the riverbanks and prison walls.

People living within five blocks of the prison were ordered to stay inside their houses unless their business was extremely urgent, and warned that they might have difficulty getting back if they left. Gasoline filling stations and small shops were ordered to close and stay closed until sunrise.

---

executions. Anticipating its findings, a strongly worded dissent appeared in the *Atlantic Monthly* magazine by Felix Frankfurter, a highly regarded faculty member of the Harvard Law School, who added his voice to the protest: "Outside the courtroom the Red hysteria was rampant; it was allowed to dominate inside."[45]

The Frankfurter article galvanized the support of respectable, educated Americans for Sacco and Vanzetti more than any other factor. Titled "The Case of Sacco and Vanzetti," the lengthy article was powerfully written, read by tens of thousands, and provided a penetrating glimpse into Frankfurter's view of general bias inherent in the American justice system as well as specific prejudices that flawed this case. More than seventy-five years after its publication, it continues to be reprinted and studied as evidence of unethical conduct within Thayer's courtroom.

Frankfurter began with a meticulous account of the case, from descriptions of the crime scene, the car, the police, and the street-car to the arrests and pretrial publicity. He then quoted extensively from the trial transcript. He specifically focused on key witnesses, apparent contradictory testimony, confusion, inappropriate questions, and questionable remarks made by witnesses,

A crowd in Boston rallies in support of Sacco and Vanzetti after their execution date is set. Many people around the world condemned the sentence as a miscarriage of justice.

Harvard law professor and future Supreme Court justice Felix Frankfurter wrote a scathing criticism of the trial. The article, however, failed to sway Judge Thayer's opinion.

attorneys, and most of all Thayer. Frankfurter then bluntly concluded what many Americans privately suspected:

> But recently facts have been disclosed, and not denied by the prosecution, to indicate that the case against these Italians for murder was part of a collusive effort between the District Attorney and agents of the Department of Justice

to rid the country of Sacco and Vanzetti because of their Red activities.[46]

He then discussed Thayer's role in the trial and statements, casting doubt on his objectivity and competency. Frankfurter spoke for many Americans when he said, "No wonder that Judge Thayer's opinion has confirmed old doubts as to the guilt of these two Italians and aroused new anxieties concerning the resources of our law to avoid grave miscarriage of justice."[47]

Frankfurter argued strongly that the more likely killers of Parmenter and Berardelli were members of the Morelli gang. He concluded that there was at least enough evidence and questionable activity to warrant retrying Sacco and Vanzetti, an opinion shared even by many who believed they were guilty.

The article added fuel to the public controversy. For the first time in a prestigious magazine by a respected faculty member of the Harvard Law School, a symbol of Old Yankee America, had arrived at the same conclusion as poor immigrants and Red activists.

The Final Flurry

Frankfurter's article may have influenced many, but it failed to sway Thayer or the Massachusetts Supreme Court. On April 5, 1927, the court handed down its final ruling rejecting the Madeiros appeal and instructed Thayer to sentence Sacco and Vanzetti and set an execution date. He did so on April 9 with the convicted men standing before him in the Dedham courthouse.

Thayer allowed each man to speak on his own behalf before he pronounced the death sentence. Both men strongly denied any guilt in the murders in South Braintree seven years earlier. Each proclaimed himself the victim of persecution in a class struggle between the rich and the oppressed. Vanzetti condemned Thayer and the defense attorneys as incompetent and insisted he would never abandon his anarchist convictions. When they finished their speeches, Thayer sentenced Sacco and Vanzetti in turn, saying to each that he would "Suffer the punishment of death by the passage of electrical current through your body. This is the sentence of the law." [48] Thayer then set the execution date for August 23, 1927.

The Sacco and Vanzetti Defense Committee issued a desperate call: "Come by train and boat, come on foot or in your car! Come to Boston! Let all the roads of the nation converge on Beacon Hill!" [49] More petitions poured into the governor's office from around the world: 474,842 names on one, 153,000 names on another. In August, hundreds of thousands of people from Boston and New York to London, Paris, and Buenos Aires took to the

Workers in London rally to save Sacco and Vanzetti from execution. Similar protests were staged around the world to no avail.

streets in protest of what they perceived to be a massive miscarriage of justice.

There was one final flurry of legal activity. On August 18, 1927, just five days before the execution date, the Massachusetts Supreme Court denied the defense's final petition for a new trial claiming Thayer had displayed prejudice against the defendants during the trial. With the scheduled execution just days away, attorneys headed for the federal courts. On August 19, a federal district judge in Boston rejected the defense petition for a writ of habeas corpus, in this case, an attempt to move the defendants out of Massachusetts. The next day, defense attorneys went to Washington, D.C., to file petitions with the U.S. Supreme Court and an application for stays of execution with Justice Holmes. Holmes rejected the request because the crime was charged under state law and tried by a state court, and he had no authority to overturn it. Holmes noted, "You don't have to convince me that the atmosphere in which these men were tried precluded a fair trial, but that is not enough to give me, a Federal judge, jurisdiction." [50] The next day Holmes was again approached and asked to stay the execution. This time he replied that he did not feel justified in doing so unless there was a reasonable chance that the U.S. Supreme Court would reverse the judgment against Sacco and Vanzetti. "This," he noted, "I can not bring myself to believe." [51] On August 21, Justices Louis D. Brandeis and Harlan Fiske Stone, speaking for the U.S. Supreme Court, also rejected applications to stay the execution. The legal battle was over.

The Executions

After six years of separation, Sacco and Vanzetti were brought together one last time in Charlestown State Prison. On August 22, the day before the execution, Western Union installed eighteen new telegraph wires to local transmission offices to handle the demands of the world press. In Charlestown, bridges were closed and the prison roped off within a one-mile radius. Machine guns were set up on the prison walls and catwalks. Patrolling the streets of Charlestown were state troopers, mounted police, rail-road police, and motorcycle officers. A crowd of several thousand people gathered in the Charlestown city square. Boston-area radio stations announced that they would remain on the air past their usual ten o'clock sign-offs to broadcast news of the midnight executions.

As midnight drew near, Sacco and Vanzetti sat in their cells awaiting the call from Warden William Hendry to take their last twelve steps to the electric chair. Hendry first summoned Sacco, who made the walk unassisted between two guards. In the death chamber, the guards strapped Sacco into the wood-and-leather

Thousands of people line the streets during Sacco and Vanzetti's funeral procession in Boston. The controversy surrounding their case did not die with them.

chair that had been set before a select group of witnesses and an Associated Press reporter. It was 12:03 A.M. Strapped to his chair, his face pale, Sacco was defiant to the end, uttering his last words in his native Italian, *"Viva l'anarchia"* ("Long live anarchy!") And then in English, "Farewell my wife and child and all my friends." Then, calmly looking at the witnesses, he said, "Good evening gentlemen." And finally, following Hendry's order to apply the electrical current, Sacco blurted, "Farewell Mother,"[52] an instant before a two-thousand-volt current passed through him.

After Sacco's body was removed, Hendry ordered Vanzetti's cell door opened. Vanzetti stood calmly and shook hands with his guards. Upon entering the execution chamber, he turned to Hendry and said in English, "I want to thank you for all you have done Warden." Then, addressing the room of witnesses, he said, "I wish to say to you that I am innocent. I have never committed any crime, but sometimes some sins. I thank you for everything you have done for me. I am innocent of all crime, not only this one, but all. I am an innocent man. I wish to forgive some people for what they are doing to me."[53]

The morning banner headline in the *New York Times* read, "Sacco and Vanzetti Put to Death Early This Morning; Governor Fuller Rejects Last Minute Plea for Delay After a Day of Legal Moves and Demonstrations."[54]

Chapter 5

The Case That
Will Not Die

THE DEBATE OVER the guilt or innocence of Sacco and Vanzetti did not end with their deaths. Since then, their case has come to be known as "the case that will not die," reflected in a stream of analyses of the trial and of one of America's darkest political eras. Controversy continues to swirl around the case, and continuing reevaluation of evidence and testimony regularly renews the debate.

At the heart of the controversy is the central question: Were Sacco and Vanzetti guilty of murder, or were they found guilty because they were radical anarchists? Surprisingly, early in the twenty-first century the prevailing view that they were framed has shifted to the view that both were probably involved in the crime.

Bullet Number III: 1961 and 1983

The single most important piece of evidence remains bullet number III. It is not surprising that refinement in ballistics testing in later decades inspired people to reexamine the focus of so much controversy. Massachusetts commissioner of public safety Frank Giles agreed to subject bullet III to another ballistics test in 1961, when compound microscopes had been developed that could compare two bullets under such high resolution that a conclusive identification was likely. The test was arranged in the ballistics laboratory at the Massachusetts Police Academy using two state-of-the-art compound microscopes just to verify the results.

Two ballistics experts, each at opposite ends of the room, independently inspected bullet number III and a test bullet fired from Sacco's gun under high magnification. Then, without revealing their findings to each other, they unfocused their microscopes, changed places, and repeated the comparison. Each submitted an affidavit stating that bullet number III had been fired by Sacco's pistol and could not have been fired by any other weapon.

In 1983, a repeat of the same test was requested by the Massachusetts State Police in response to continuing calls to reevaluate the evidence in the case. The results were identical to the two previous tests. When asked to comment about the outcome, head

THE INTELLECTUAL COMMUNITY'S RESPONSE

Many within the American intellectual community expressed their outrage at the Sacco and Vanzetti convictions and executions in books, poetry, plays, and music. All denounced the executions as a reflection of America's morally corrupt industrial society, government, and judiciary. One of the most impassioned, writer John Dos Passos, expressed in his book *USA* his indignation at the execution of Sacco and Vanzetti and how it divided the nation:

Author John Dos Passos was outraged by the Sacco and Vanzetti conviction.

> They have clubbed us off the streets they are stronger they are rich they hire and fire the politicians the newspaper editors the old judges.

> They hire the men with guns the uniforms the police cars the patrol wagons.

> All right you have won you will kill the brave men our friends tonight there is nothing left to do we are beaten.

They have built the electric chair and hired the executioner to throw the switch all right we are two nations.

examiner Marshall Robinson replied, "Why do they keep running these tests over and over? They always come out the same."[55]

But dispute over hard evidence alone could not have fueled the debate over four generations. Many noted writers have taken up the cause of Sacco and Vanzetti on political grounds. One work in particular, Felix Frankfurter's argument that Sacco and Vanzetti were unjustly convicted, became even more influential when Frankfurter was appointed to the U.S. Supreme Court in 1939. During his twenty-three-year tenure on the Court, he distinguished himself as a fair, progressive jurist and an eloquent writer. His advocacy of Sacco and Vanzetti lent a great deal of authority to their defenders' case.

Confessions Following the Executions

Confessions also keep the Sacco and Vanzetti debate alive. Years after the executions, many who knew the two men and many others who claimed to have information about the robbery and murders informally began to talk. Both sides of the continuing debate have seized on confessions as irrefutable support for their opposing positions.

The most damaging confession implicating Sacco came from anarchist leader Carlo Tresca in 1941. Tresca, the leading anarchist in Boston, had known Sacco and Vanzetti and had contributed to their legal defense fund. Two years before his own unsolved murder in 1943, he provided the first inside confirmation of Sacco's guilt when he told Communist writer Max Eastman, "Sacco was guilty but Vanzetti was innocent."[56] Eastman did not publish an account of his conversation with Tresca until 1961, but others who had known Tresca confirmed they were told the same thing.

Paul Avrich, author of *Anarchist Voices: An Oral History of Anarchism in America*, interviewed 180 former anarchists about the Sacco and Vanzetti trial and found that the question of guilt and innocence lingered. Writer Charles A. Zappia notes of Avrich's research:

> The respondents are divided on the enduring controversy over Sacco and Vanzetti's guilt, demonstrating essentially the same divisions as contemporary scholars. Most are

A detective examines the murdered body of anarchist Carlo Tresca. In 1941, two years before Tresca's death, he alleged that Sacco was guilty, but Vanzetti was innocent.

convinced that the men were innocent of the crimes for which they were executed; however, some claim that Sacco was guilty of the shooting, some that he was guilty of the robbery only. According to others, Vanzetti was either completely uninvolved, absent from the scene but possessing prior knowledge that the holdup was about to occur, or on the scene but uninvolved in the shooting. After having read all of the appropriate comments in *Anarchist Voices*, one closes the book without resolving the Sacco and Vanzetti case.[57]

Acquaintances of Sacco and Vanzetti are not the only ones to contribute inside information about the trial. Distant supporters of Sacco and Vanzetti point to a variety of off-the-record comments casting doubt on Thayer's and the jury's objectivity. One reporter decided to interview the jury himself.

Jurists' Reflections

After the verdict, Judge Thayer thanked the twelve jurors for their service and released them to go home. All eagerly returned to their jobs and families and resumed normal lives. Some experienced occasional taunting by supporters of Sacco and Vanzetti and outright scorn by writers expressing a bias in favor of the two

Vanzetti and Sacco sit handcuffed to a guard during their trial. Criticisms of the trial's proceedings continued to appear years after the defendants were executed.

anarchists. But as time passed, most of the tension dissipated and the identity of the jurors faded from public memory.

Criticism of the trial, however, did not dissipate. In an attempt to evaluate the fairness of the trial, the *New Bedford Standard-Times* newspaper feature writer Edward Simmons interviewed seven surviving jurors in 1950. He was interested in comparing their feelings about the trial in 1921 with their opinions nearly three decades later. Simmons asked each man if he felt the trial had been conducted in a fair and impartial manner or not, and whether Judge Thayer's court conduct had been evenhanded.

According to juror John Dever, the verdict was a logical conclusion based on hard evidence:

> It is nonsense to say we were prejudiced against Sacco and Vanzetti because they were Italian and anarchists. . . . Various pieces [of evidence] fitted into the chains of evidence, which to my mind, not having a weak link, were pretty strong. I was a defendant's man all the way through the trial. I don't mean I was determined to vote for their innocence regardless, but I was going to find them not guilty until the facts proved otherwise to my definite satisfaction. [58]

Four other jurors—George Gerard, Frank Marden, John Ganley, and Seward Parker—gave Simmons the following four responses:

> The outstanding thing about the trial was the Judge. The fairest Judge I ever saw or heard of.

> I have never had a bit of reason to think the trial was anything but fair. I don't think we jurors thought of the defendants in any way except as to persons accused of murder.

> Thayer was absolutely fearless and absolutely on the level. He was trying to do his job thoroughly and not leaning either way.

> Why should we want to pick up two Reds and try to convict them of murder? To my mind, and I really think this,

the Judge really tried to help the defendants. He was square with us too. . . . I had no difficulty in my own mind arriving at the verdict. . . . If I remember anything with absolute clarity, it was the judge's fairness. [59]

In 1961, David Felix, author of *Protest: Sacco and Vanzetti and the Intellectuals*, interviewed juror Harry King, who was then living in Boston. Reflecting back forty years, King had a clear conscience about the verdict the jury rendered:

I know there was a lot of talk about it afterward, radicalism and all that. The jury didn't mention it when we discussed the evidence. . . . I'm a church member. I was a deacon then. I wouldn't make a decision about a man's life unless I was sure I was doing right. Well, I have no regrets about the decision—only that I was picked to make it. [60]

The Gambera Letter

The most intriguing piece of information brought to light in recent years was mailed to the Cape Cod home of historian Francis Russell in November 1982. Russell, who had published a book on the case, *Tragedy in Dedham: The Story of the Sacco and Vanzetti Case*, received an unsolicited two-page letter from Ideale Gambera, son of Giovanni Gambera. The elder Gambera had been one of a few avowed anarchists close to both Sacco and Vanzetti before, during, and following their trial. In the letter, the son explained that because his father had died, it was now possible to reveal information formerly held in strictest secrecy:

Everyone [in the Boston anarchist circle] knew that Sacco was guilty and that Vanzetti was innocent as far as the actual participation in the killing. But no one would ever break the code of silence, even if it cost Vanzetti's life. My father was in the case from its beginning but is never mentioned simply because that is the way he wished it. He commanded great respect and loyalty amongst the anarchists combined with an aura of deadly intent. He was head of a family of six and he was involved in so

Modern Analyses

A review of recent literature documenting the trial of Sacco and Vanzetti reveals a range of analyses from responsible fact finding to the irrational and absurd. One of the more extreme examples can be found in the book *After Twelve Years*, by assistant defense attorneys Michael Angel Musmanno, who reminisced about the trial: "It began with that hick cop Stewart in Bridgewater, you've got to understand that to understand anything else. With his crazy Irish imagination he started it all! You know what he said right after he found the Buick? 'The man who did this job knew no God.' Every atheist is a suspect. Without that hick cop weaving his fantasies there never would have been a Sacco-Vanzetti case."

Another statement, part of a fifty-year anniversary observation of the executions, appearing in the *Atlantic Monthly* in June 1977 titled "The Never-Ending Wrong," was written by novelist Katherine Anne Porter. Porter makes the following off-handed comparison between Nazi Germany and the American judicial system as represented by Judge Thayer:

> During Hitler's time, Himmler [head of the Nazi secret police] remarked that for the good of the state, popular complaints should be ignored, and if they persisted, the complainers should be punished. Judge Webster Thayer, during the Sacco-Vanzetti episode, was heard to boast while playing golf, "Did you see what I did to those anarchistic bastards?"

In 1939 defense attorney Michael Angel Musmanno published a book criticizing the trial as a travesty of justice.

many activities of dubious nature that he made sure that no disgrace of notoriety would touch us.[61]

The letter goes on to say,

Before [the Braintree murders and arrests of Sacco and Vanzetti] all became public, there was a committee of four who represented Sacco and Vanzetti. These four were Aldono Felicani, Professor Guadagni, Lucia Mancini, and my father. The prime purpose of this committee was to decide what should happen to Sacco and Vanzetti.[62]

Russell considered this letter one of the two most compelling development—the modern ballistics tests being the other—in the case since the time of the executions. Till this point Russell had been convinced by the evidence that Sacco and Vanzetti had been unjustly tried and executed. These two pieces of new evidence, however, changed his opinion; his more recent book, *Sacco & Vanzetti: The Case Resolved*, reflects the view that Sacco was definitely one of the killers and that Vanzetti was involved but not a killer.

A Few Informal Candid Remarks

Letters written by major figures in the case have come to light in the years following the trial. Although never intended for publication, several provide personal glimpses into the trial and at times change people's perception of the proceedings leading up to the trial. Years following the trial, Moore admitted that the prosecution had a much stronger case against Sacco than against Vanzetti. According to Douglas Linder of the University of Missouri–Kansas City School of Law, Moore recounted in a letter to American writer Upton Sinclair how tempted he was, in his summation, to stress the weakness of the evidence against Vanzetti:

There was so little evidence against Vanzetti—almost none in fact—I believed that there was a good chance of acquittal if I should push home the fact. But I felt sure, in that case, Sacco would be found guilty. I thought there was a fighting chance the jury would disagree as to the two but if they acquitted one I knew enough of juries to feel sure

Harvard University president A. Lawrence Lowell headed the governor's committee that vindicated the verdict in the Sacco and Vanzetti case.

they would soak the other. So I put it to Vanzetti: "What shall I do?" and he answered, "Save Nick, he has the woman and child." [63]

The Lowell Report was similarly scrutinized. Many people interpreted the Lowell Report as firmly supporting the guilt of Sacco but hinting at some uncertainty as to Vanzetti's guilt. According to Linder, however, Lowell rejected that suggestion in a letter to a friend in England. Although he admitted the case against Vanzetti was wholly circumstantial, the final impression of the commission "was that Vanzetti was the plotter and Sacco an executioner." [64]

Jailhouse Letters of Sacco and Vanzetti

During their seven years in prison, both Sacco and Vanzetti were prolific letter writers. When their letters to friends and family were first published one year after their deaths, readers were struck by the depth of their commitment to anarchism as well as by their eloquence, devotion to family, and love of life.

THE DUKAKIS PROCLAMATION

A rather unusual example of how the Sacco and Vanzetti trial continues to be "the case that will not die" can be found in a proclamation issued by Michael Dukakis, former governor of Massachusetts. On August 23, 1977, the fiftieth anniversary of the execution, the governor dedicated the day to the pair. He did not specify his motives for this proclamation, which was not a post-mortem pardon, and skeptics dismissed the proclamation as merely a play to garner Italian votes for his approaching reelection. Regardless, the proclamation highlights some of the manifestations of the Red Scare. An excerpt, reprinted in *Postmortem: New Evidence in the Case of Sacco and Vanzetti*, by William Young and David E. Kaiser, follows:

Michael Dukakis declared August 23, 1977, Sacco and Vanzetti day.

I, Michael S. Dukakis, Governor of the Commonwealth of Massachusetts, by virtue of the authority conferred upon me as Supreme Executive Magistrate by the Constitution of the Commonwealth of Massachusetts, and by all other authority vested in me, do hereby proclaim Tuesday, August 23, 1977, "NICOLA SACCO AND BARTOLOMEO VANZETTI MEMORIAL DAY"; and declare, further, that any stigma and disgrace should be forever removed from the names of Nicola Sacco and Bartolomeo Vanzetti, from the names of their families and descendants, and so, from the name of the Commonwealth of Massachusetts; and I hereby call upon all the people of Massachusetts to pause in their daily endeavors to reflect upon these tragic events, and draw from their historic lessons the resolve to prevent the forces of intolerance, fear, and hatred from ever again uniting to overcome rationality, wisdom, and fairness to which our legal system aspires.

Many readers of their letters were persuaded that men so passionate about life and family could not possibly be murderers. Others believed the calm with which Sacco and Vanzetti accepted their deaths was a sign of their innocence and enhanced their image as martyrs of the anarchist cause.

Of the many letters they wrote, two are considered exemplary expressions of their innermost convictions and innocence. The first, which Vanzetti read aloud at his sentencing in 1927, expresses his sense of suffering, his innocence, the conviction that he will die because of his radical politics, and that he would live his life again unchanged if afforded the opportunity:

> I would not wish to a dog or to a snake, to the most low and misfortunate creature of the earth—I would not wish to any of them what I have had to suffer for things that I am not guilty of. But my conviction is that I have suffered for things I am guilty of. I am suffering because I am a radical and indeed I am a radical; I have suffered because I was an Italian, and indeed I am an Italian; I have suffered more for my family and for my beloved than for myself; but I am so convinced to be right that if you could execute me two times, and if I could be reborn two other times, I would live again to do what I have done already. [65]

In April 1927, Sacco sent the following letter to Phillip Strong, a reporter for the North American Newspaper Alliance. Speaking for himself and on behalf of Vanzetti, Sacco poetically expresses the strength that he has gained knowing that he will die for a worthy cause:

> If it had not been for these things, I might have live out my life talking at street corners to scorning men. I might have die, unmarked, unknown, a failure. Now we are not a failure. This is our career and our triumph. Never in our full life can we hope to do such work for tolerance for joostice [justice], for man's understanding of man is now [what] we do by accident. Our words—our lives—our

In 1999 Sacco and Vanzetti's death masks and ashes are displayed at the Boston Public Library. The controversy surrounding the trial continues to intrigue people.

pains—nothing! The taking of our lives—lives of a good shoemaker and a fish peddler—all! That last triumph belongs to us—that agony is our triumph. [66]

The Trial's Modern-Day Relevance

In 1977, to commemorate the fiftieth anniversary of the executions, Massachusetts governor Michael Dukakis signed a proclamation noting the historical event. Since that proclamation, at least six major books and dozens of short articles about Sacco and Vanzetti have appeared in print. Ongoing interest such as this continues to elevate a simple case of murder into one of the great trials of the twentieth century. At the heart of the interest is the way the trial exposed some of the shortcomings of the American judicial system. While the courtroom is ideally an island of impartiality and fairness, in all historical periods, strong political currents, including xenophobia and antiradical sentiment, are reflected in judicial proceedings.

The trial occurred in an America swept up by the twin fears of political and social instability following World War I. These fears, justified by threats to overthrow the government and bombs exploding across the nation, translated into a fear of immigrants with questionable loyalties on the part of a few and sometimes antidemocratic politics. The result was the hysteria of the Red Scare led by Attorney General Palmer, who sought to calm America's collective fears by curtailing civil liberties and through questionable scare tactics.

The controversy remains relevant as the United States continues to welcome immigrants while grappling with complex problems of balancing their civil liberties against the threats of terrorism. Xenophobia, patriotism, and assimilation issues are at the center of political debate today, just as they were in 1920.

Notes

Introduction: Politics on Trial

1. *New York Times*, June 3, 1919, p. A1.
2. Quoted in Ted DeCorte, "The Red Scare 1919–1920," *Port Townsend and Jefferson County Leader*, 1979. www.ptleader.com.

Chapter 1: The Crime and the Investigation

3. *Boston Herald*, April 16, 1920.
4. Quoted in Francis Russell, *Sacco & Vanzetti: The Case Resolved*. New York: Harper & Row, 1986, pp. 61–62.
5. Quoted in Herbert B. Ehrmann, *The Case That Will Not Die: Commonwealth vs. Sacco & Vanzetti*. New York: Little, Brown, 1969, pp. 54–55.
6. *Boston Herald*, May 7, 1920.
7. Quoted in Francis Russell, *Tragedy in Dedham: The Story of the Sacco and Vanzetti Case*. New York: McGraw-Hill, 1962, p. 107.
8. Anonymous archival photograph, *Daily Bleed*, www.eskimo.com/~recall/bleed/0714.htm.

Chapter 2: The Prosecution: The Case for Old Yankee America

9. Quoted in Ehrmann, *The Case That Will Not Die*, p. 160.
10. Quoted in Douglas Linder, "The Trial of Sacco and Vanzetti," School of Law, University of Missouri–Kansas City, 2001. www.law.umkc.edu.
11. *Transcript of the Record of the Trial of Nicola Sacco and Bartolomeo Vanzetti in the Courts of Massachusetts and Subsequent Proceedings, 1920–1927*, Mamaroneck, NY: Appel, 1969, p. 337.
12. *Transcript of the Record of the Trial of Nicola Sacco and Bartolomeo Vanzetti, 1920–1927*, p. 209.
13. *Transcript of the Record of the Trial of Nicola Sacco and Bartolomeo Vanzetti, 1920–1927*, p. 1,728.
14. *Transcript of the Record of the Trial of Nicola Sacco and Bartolomeo Vanzetti, 1920–1927*, p. 1,728.
15. *Transcript of the Record of the Trial of Nicola Sacco and Bartolomeo Vanzetti, 1920–1927*, p. 1,733.

16. *Transcript of the Record of the Trial of Nicola Sacco and Bartolomeo Vanzetti, 1920–1927*, p. 1,867.
17. *Transcript of the Record of the Trial of Nicola Sacco and Bartolomeo Vanzetti, 1920–1927*, p. 1,733.
18. *Transcript of the Record of the Trial of Nicola Sacco and Bartolomeo Vanzetti, 1920–1927*, p. 1,734.

Chapter 3: The Defense: Blaming Red Scare Hysteria

19. Russell, *Tragedy in Dedham*, p. 110.
20. *Transcript of the Record of the Trial of Nicola Sacco and Bartolomeo Vanzetti, 1920–1927*, p. 2,133.
21. *Transcript of the Record of the Trial of Nicola Sacco and Bartolomeo Vanzetti, 1920–1927*, p. 1,738.
22. *Transcript of the Record of the Trial of Nicola Sacco and Bartolomeo Vanzetti, 1920–1927*, p. 1,744.
23. *Transcript of the Record of the Trial of Nicola Sacco and Bartolomeo Vanzetti, 1920–1927*, p. 1,744.
24. *Transcript of the Record of the Trial of Nicola Sacco and Bartolomeo Vanzetti, 1920–1927*, p. 1,751.
25. Quoted in Henry Lee and Jerry Labriola, *Famous Crimes Revisited: From Sacco and Vanzetti to O. J. Simpson.* Southington, CT: Strong Books, 2001, p. 56.
26. Quoted in Lee and Labriola, *Famous Crimes Revisited*, p. 57.
27. *Transcript of the Record of the Trial of Nicola Sacco and Bartolomeo Vanzetti, 1920–1927*, p. 2,128.
28. *Transcript of the Record of the Trial of Nicola Sacco and Bartolomeo Vanzetti, 1920–1927*, p. 2,178.
29. *Transcript of the Record of the Trial of Nicola Sacco and Bartolomeo Vanzetti, 1920–1927*, p. 2,225.
30. *Transcript of the Record of the Trial of Nicola Sacco and Bartolomeo Vanzetti, 1920–1927*, p. 2,237.
31. *Transcript of the Record of the Trial of Nicola Sacco and Bartolomeo Vanzetti, 1920–1927*, p. 2,241.
32. *Transcript of the Record of the Trial of Nicola Sacco and Bartolomeo Vanzetti, 1920–1927*, p. 2,264.
33. *Transcript of the Record of the Trial of Nicola Sacco and Bartolomeo Vanzetti, 1920–1927*, p. 2,265.

34. *Transcript of the Record of the Trial of Nicola Sacco and Bartolomeo Vanzetti, 1920–1927*, p. 2,266.

35. Quoted in Russell, *Tragedy in Dedham*, p. 214.

36. Quoted in Russell, *Tragedy in Dedham*, p. 214.

37. Quoted in Russell, *Tragedy in Dedham*, p. 214.

Chapter 4: The Fight to Escape the Electric Chair

38. *Transcript of the Record of the Trial of Nicola Sacco and Bartolomeo Vanzetti, 1920–1927*, p. 3,580.

39. *Transcript of the Record of the Trial of Nicola Sacco and Bartolomeo Vanzetti, 1920–1927*, p. 1,728.

40. Quoted in "The Commonwealth of Massachusetts vs. Sacco and Vanzetti: The Ballistic Evidence," The Atlantic Online, 2001. www.theatlantic.com.

41. Quoted in Robert Weeks, *Commonwealth vs. Sacco and Vanzetti*. Englewood Cliffs, NJ: Prentice-Hall, 1958, p. 205.

42. *Transcript of the Record of the Trial of Nicola Sacco and Bartolomeo Vanzetti, 1920–1927*, p. 4,727.

43. Quoted in Linder, "The Trial of Sacco and Vanzetti."

44. Quoted in Robert D'Attilio, "SACCO-VANZETTI CASE," The English Department at the University of Pennsylvania, 1999. www.english.upenn.edu.

45. Felix Frankfurter, "The Case of Sacco and Vanzetti," *Atlantic Monthly*, March 27, 1927, p. 23.

46. Frankfurter, "The Case of Sacco and Vanzetti," p. 43.

47. Frankfurter, "The Case of Sacco and Vanzetti," p. 52.

48. *Transcript of the Record of the Trial of Nicola Sacco and Bartolomeo Vanzetti, 1920–1927*, p. 4,905.

49. Quoted in Linder, "The Trial of Sacco and Vanzetti."

50. Quoted in Russell, *Tragedy in Dedham*, p. 423.

51. Quoted in Russell, *Tragedy in Dedham*, p. 434.

52. Quoted in Weeks, *Commonwealth vs. Sacco and Vanzetti*, p. 150.

53. Quoted in Weeks, *Commonwealth vs. Sacco and Vanzetti*, p. 151.

54. *New York Times*, August 23, 1927, p. A1.

Chapter 5: The Case That Will Not Die

55. Quoted in Russell, *Sacco & Vanzetti*, p. 161.

56. Quoted in Russell, *Sacco & Vanzetti*, p. 27.

57. Charles A. Zappia, "Memories of American Anarchism," H-Net: Humanities and Social Sciences Online, www.h-net.org.

58. Quoted in Russell, *Sacco & Vanzetti*, p. 112.

59. Quoted in Russell, *Sacco & Vanzetti*, p. 112.

60. Quoted in Russell, *Sacco & Vanzetti*, p. 112.

61. Russell, *Sacco & Vanzetti*, pp. 12–13.

62. Russell, *Sacco & Vanzetti*, p. 13.

63. Quoted in Linder, "The Trial of Sacco and Vanzetti."

64. Quoted in Linder, "The Trial of Sacco and Vanzetti."

65. Quoted in Juliet Ucelli, "Sacco & Vanzetti Commemoration Speech," 1977, www.italianamericanwriters.com.

66. Quoted in Marion Frankfurter and Gardner Jackson, *The Letters of Sacco and Vanzetti*. New York: E.P. Dutton, 1960, p. v.

For Further Reading

Books

John Dos Passos, *USA*. New York: Modern Library, 1936. This work is a trilogy documenting, in fictional form, Dos Passos's view of American life during the post–World War I era.

Nancy Gentile Ford, *Americans All! Foreign-Born Soldiers in World War I*. College Station: Texas A&M University Press, 2001. The book is a good blend of the social and military history of World War I. Ford presents the history of immigrants who fought during World War I and documents the army's modernization during the war to accommodate the half million foreign-born soldiers from forty-six different countries. She documents the army's efforts to teach them English, the basics of American culture, and how to socialize with American troops.

Felix Frankfurter, *The Case of Sacco and Vanzetti: A Critical Analysis for Lawyers and Laymen*. Boston: Little, Brown, 1927. This book is largely an elaboration of his article, "The Case of Sacco and Vanzetti," published the same year in the *Atlantic Monthly* magazine. Frankfurter's book reflects his conviction that Sacco and Vanzetti were falsely accused and unfairly tried. Reviews of his book following its publication ranged from adulation to condemnation, depending upon the reviewer's analysis of the trial.

Marion Frankfurter and Gardner Jackson, *The Letters of Sacco and Vanzetti*. New York: E.P. Dutton, 1960. This book contains the letters Sacco and Vanzetti wrote in jail over the seven years following their conviction while awaiting execution. Their letters speak of many things, ranging from the trial, departing Italy, anarchy, and their families. These sensitive and sometimes poetic letters are often cited as evidence that neither man could have committed the murders.

Emma Goldman, *Living My Life*. New York: Dover, 1970. Goldman's autobiography provides an excellent history of her radical politics and militant activism in America and Russia. A prominent anarchist, she wrote about her deportation on the SS

Buford in 1920. In addition, her work highlights her social commitment to woman's rights and the rights of workers.

Henry Lee and Jerry Labriola, *Famous Crimes Revisited: From Sacco and Vanzetti to O. J. Simpsom.* Southington, CT: Strong Books, 2001. A study of several of the most well-documented trials of the twentieth century, this book dedicates seven chapters to the Sacco and Vanzetti case.

Robert H. Montgomery, *Sacco and Vanzetti: The Murder and the Myth.* New York: Devin-Adair, 1960. Montgomery's book provides a good history of the trial concluding that the ballistics evidence points to both men as participants in the murders in South Braintree.

William Young and David E. Kaiser, *Postmortem: New Evidence in the Case of Sacco and Vanzetti.* Amherst: University of Massachusetts Press, 1985. The two authors reexamine the 1921 murder case that resulted in the execution of Sacco and Vanzetti, and make the case that based on new evidence and testimony, the two men were most likely framed for murders they did not commit. This work is not considered a reliable account by most historians of the trial.

Web Sites

Court TV (www.courttv.com). This site, which is maintained by the television network of the same name, provides a series of links to many of the great American trials. For the Sacco and Vanzetti case, the site provides a database of historical information that includes a good background to the trial, the trial itself, and its aftermath to the present.

The Sacco Vanzetti Project (www.saccovanzettiproject.org). This site provides a wealth of documentation for the Sacco and Vanzetti trial that includes photographs, newspaper headlines, political cartoons, letters, and a bibliography of books written on the trial and its aftermath.

School of Law, University of Missouri–Kansas City (www.law. umkc.edu). This is a law school Web site that provides a database of information for many of the most famous trials in American jurisprudence. Its information on the Sacco and Vanzetti trial is clear and easy to access and understand.

Works Consulted

Books

Paul Avrich, *Anarchist Voices: An Oral History of Anarchism in America.* Princeton, NJ: Princeton University Press, 1995. This book contains 180 interviews of anarchists conducted by Avrich over a period of thirty years. Most of the interviewees were active between the 1880s and the 1930s. The interviews include minor figures as well as the major ones such as Emma Goldman and Sacco and Vanzetti.

———, *Sacco and Vanzetti: The Anarchist Background.* Princeton, NJ: Princeton University Press, 1991. Although the title makes the book appear to be about Sacco and Vanzetti, it is actually focused on Galleanists, the followers of Italian anarchist Luigi Galleani, who defined his radical form of anarchy with a series of violent bombings. Avrich points out that these bombings played a major role in America's period of the Red Scare.

Herbert B. Ehrmann, *The Case That Will Not Die: Commonwealth vs. Sacco & Vanzetti.* New York: Little, Brown, 1969. Ehrmann was the last living lawyer involved in the Sacco and Vanzetti case during the writing of this book. He represented Sacco and Vanzetti. It is a voluminous work, nearly six hundred pages, encompassing all aspects of the crime, politics, and trial. In this respect, the book is extremely informative. Unfortunately, however, the book is also highly prejudicial, proposing that Sacco and Vanzetti were yet another example of how governments oppress and murder innocent citizens.

Roberta Strauss Feuerlicht, *Justice Crucified: The Story of Sacco and Vanzetti.* New York: McGraw-Hill, 1977. This work is widely considered the least respected of the Sacco and Vanzetti books. It provides a broad history of the trial but attacks the mechanics of the trial and its outcome without providing adequate documentation to support the author's highly biased claims of a conspiracy against the defendants.

Luigi Galleani, *The End of Anarchism?*, trans. Max Sartin and Robert D'Attilio. Minneapolis, MN: Cienfuegos Press, 1982.

This work is a compilation of hundreds of Galleani's anarchist writings over a thirty-year period.

Francis Russell, *Tragedy in Dedham: The Story of the Sacco and Vanzetti Case*. New York: McGraw-Hill, 1962. The first of Russell's two major works about the trial, this one provides an excellent history concluding that Sacco and Vanzetti were falsely charged and that a new trial would have exonerated the two.

———, *Sacco & Vanzetti: The Case Resolved*. New York: Harper & Row, 1986. The second of Russell's two major works about the trial, this book concludes that recent evidence in the form of an anarchist's confession and modern ballistics evidence proves both Sacco and Vanzetti were involved in the killings.

Transcript of the Record of the Trial of Nicola Sacco and Bartolomeo Vanzetti in the Courts of Massachusetts and Subsequent Proceedings, 1920–1927. Mamaroneck, NY: Appel, 1969. This six-volume work is the official transcript of the Sacco and Vanzetti trial and all appeals.

Trustees of the Public Library of the City of Boston, *Sacco-Vanzetti: Developments and Reconsiderations—1979*. Boston: Boston Public Library, 1982. This book, sponsored by the Boston Public Library, is a compillation of presentations made by several writers sympathetic to the deaths of Sacco and Vanzetti at the fiftieth anniversary of their executions.

Robert Weeks, *Commonwealth vs. Sacco and Vanzetti*. Englewood Cliffs, NJ: Prentice-Hall, 1958. This is an excellent shortened version of the lengthy official transcript. Weeks selects what he believes is the most interesting and pertinent court testimony.

Periodicals

Boston Herald, April 16, 1920.

Boston Herald, May 7, 1920.

Felix Frankfurter, "The Case of Sacco and Vanzetti," *Atlantic Monthly*, March 27, 1927.

New York Times, June 3, 1919.

New York Times, August 23, 1927.

Katherine Anne Porter, "The Never-Ending Wrong," *Atlantic Monthly*, June 1977.

Internet Sources

Anonymous archival photograph, *Daily Bleed*, www.eskimo.com/~ recall/bleed/0714.htm.

"The Commonwealth of Massachusetts vs. Sacco and Vanzetti: The Ballistic Evidence," The Atlantic Online, 2001. www.the atlantic.com.

Robert D'Attilio, "SACCO-VANZETTI CASE," The English Department at the University of Pennsylvania, 1999. www. english.upenn.edu.

Ted DeCorte, "The Red Scare 1919–1920," *Port Townsend and Jefferson County Leader,* 1979. www.ptleader.com.

Richard Johnson, "John Dos Passos," Cal Poly Pomona, 1999. www. csupomona.edu.

Douglas Linder, "The Trial of Sacco and Vanzetti," Jurist: University of Pittsburgh School of Law, May 2001. www.jurist.law. pitt.edu.

———, "The Trial of Sacco and Vanzetti," School of Law, University of Missouri–Kansas City, 2001. www.law.umkc.edu.

"Preamble to the Constitution of the American Legion," The American Legion, 2003. www.legion.org.

Juliet Ucelli, "Sacco & Vanzetti Commemoration Speech," 1977. www.italianamericanwriters.com.

Ken Verdoia, "Wobblies," KUED The University of Utah, www. kued.org.

"Warren G. Harding," The White House, 2001. www.whitehouse. gov.

Charles A. Zappia, "Memories of American Anarchism," H-Net: Humanities and Social Sciences Online. www.h-net.org.

Index

Picture Credits

About the Author

James Barter received his undergraduate degree in history and classics at the University of California, Berkeley, followed by graduate studies in ancient history and archaeology at the University of Pennsylvania. He has taught history as well as Latin and Greek. As a Fulbright scholar at the American Academy in Rome, Barter worked on archaeological sites in and around the city as well as on sites in the Naples area. He also has worked and traveled extensively in Greece. He currently resides in Rancho Santa Fe, California.